LAKE FISHING IN VIRGINIA

BOB GOOCH

Lake Fishing in Virginia

University of Virginia Press • Charlottesville and London

University of Virginia Press

© 2004 by the Rector and Visitors of the University of Virginia

Printed in the United States of America on acid-free paper

First published 2004

9 8 7 6 5 4 3 2 1

Library of Congress Cataloging-in-Publication Data

Gooch, Bob, 1919–
   Lake fishing in Virginia / Bob Gooch.
      p.   cm.
   Includes index.
   ISBN 0-8139-2286-0 (pbk. : alk. paper)
   1. Fishing—Virginia—Guidebooks.   2. Lakes—Virginia—
Guidebooks.   3. Virginia—Guidebooks.   I. Title.
   SH557.G659 2004
   799.1'1'09755—dc22

                                        2004008108

Contents

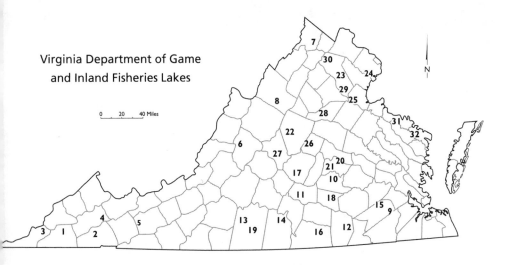

Virginia Department of Game
and Inland Fisheries Lakes

0   20   40 Miles

SOUTHWEST
1. Bark Camp Lake
2. Hidden Valley Lake
3. Keokee Lake
4. Laurel Bed Lake
5. Rural Retreat Lake

**NORTHWEST MOUNTAINS
AND VALLEY**
6. Lake A. Willis Robertson
7. Lake Frederick
8. Lake Shenandoah

SOUTHSIDE
9. Lake Airfield
10. Lake Amelia
11. Briery Creek Lake
12. Lake Brunswick
13. Lake Burton
14. Lake Conner
15. Game Refuge Lake
16. Lake Gordon

17. Horsepen Lake
18. Lake Nottoway
19. Pete's Pond
20. Powhatan Lakes
21. Powhatan Ponds

PIEDMONT
22. Lake Albemarle
23. Lake Brittle
24. Burke Lake
25. Lake Curtis
26. Fluvanna Ruritan Lake
27. Lake Nelson
28. Lake Orange
29. Phelps Pond
30. Lake Thompson

NORTHERN NECK
31. Chandler's Millpond
32. Gardy's Millpond

Introduction

The fisheries biologists of the Virginia Department of Game and Inland Fisheries manage thousands of acres of still waters for fishing. Among the larger ones are 50,000-acre Buggs Island Lake and 20,000-acre Smith Mountain Lake, but there are many smaller waters such as those in the state parks. Virginia is rich in impounded still waters. The state actually has only two natural lakes, Lake Drummond in the Great Dismal Swamp National Wildlife Refuge and Mountain Lake in Giles County. Neither is a prime fishing lake, and they receive little or no attention from the department's fisheries managers.

Many of the state's still-water lakes serve multiple needs, such as flood control, hydroelectric power, and recreation. But other lakes, most of which are fairly small by comparison, are managed specifically for fishing. All are owned by the Department of Game and Inland Fisheries. Swimming, sailing, paddleboats, hunting, and for the most part gasoline motors are prohibited, though in a few of the larger lakes gasoline motors of 10 horsepower or less are permitted. Electric motors, however, are allowed.

In some rare cases where the fish population becomes too unbalanced, a lake is drained. The undesirable fish are removed, and it is then refilled and stocked with desirable fish.

The department built dams and impounded many of these lakes, though some were built by other interests and either transferred or sold to the department to be managed for fishing. In a number of cases, landowners donated the land, desiring to have a good fishing lake for local people. There are currently thirty-two of these lakes scattered across Virginia. Modern fisheries management tools such as fertilizing the waters, monitoring the fish populations, and adjusting fishing regulations as the needs of the population demand are employed by professional fisheries managers whose training and experience rank them among the best in America.

Some of the lakes are very small, such as 3-acre Phelps Pond in Fauquier County. Briery Creek Lake in Prince Edward County at 845 acres is the largest. Many are in the 50- to 150-acre range, but size is not a true measure of the fishing opportunities. All offer good fishing.

Most offer warmwater fishing for such species as largemouth bass and bluegills, pretty much a staple in all of them. Others also offer both black and white crappie, bullhead and channel catfish, chain and redfin pickerel, fliers, northern pike in a few instances, pumpkinseed, redear and redbreast sunfish, smallmouth bass in at least one lake, muskellunge in a few lakes, walleye, warmouth, white bass, yellow perch, and possibly white bass. Several of the high-elevation lakes offer fishing for brook, brown, and rainbow trout. In other words, if a fish swims in Virginia's inland waters, you can probably find it in one of the department lakes.

These lakes are open to fishing 24 hours a day and all year. Ice fishing is popular on some of the northern lakes during many cold winters. There is no charge for fishing them—except for the cost of a state fishing license.

The lakes were built or purchased with fishing license revenues, and fishing is the primary goal. No general fund money was used to build or purchase these lakes, nor are such funds used to manage them.

A few activities other than fishing are permitted. Launching a canoe or light boat to be propelled by a paddle or electric motor is permitted. This is a possibility for bird or nature watchers who want to cruise the shoreline quietly, being careful not to disturb anglers, particularly those fishing the shoreline. In most instances the department owns 50 feet of the land back from the edge of the water so there is room for hiking or picnicking. Trails circle a few of the lakes, but at most it is simply a matter of taking off across country. In some instances there are picnic tables. In some cases there are also restrooms, particularly where there are concessions. The concessions usually offer light snacks, fishing tackle and bait, and rental boats. All but two of the very small lakes or ponds have boat-launching ramps—usually of concrete. Several also offer fishing piers and in a few instances pier facilities for those who are physically handicapped.

Primarily, however, these are fishing lakes, thirty-two of them in all, and they are scattered across Virginia. If you want to go fishing, you can be sure there is a well-managed fishing lake nearby.

The Northern Neck

THE COUNTIES OF King George, Lancaster, Northumberland, Richmond, and Westmoreland

The Northern Neck is a unique part of Virginia. It rests between the Potomac River to the north and the Rappahannock River to the south. The Chesapeake Bay forms its eastern border, and to the west it ends with the city of Fredericksburg. Both the Potomac River and the Rappahannock River are broad tidal rivers by the time they reach the Northern Neck region, but far to the west they originate as freshwater streams. The Potomac River is owned by the state of Maryland, but thanks to an agreement between the two states, licensed Virginia anglers can fish in it.

Historically rich, this is a relatively small region of gently rolling hills, marshes, timberlands, and many acres of flatlands. Despite the generally flat terrain, many deep wooded ravines or valleys ribbon it. The waters of the two big rivers vary from salt water as they enter the Chesapeake Bay to brackish and fresh as you move upstream. Inland freshwater is limited to creeks or small streams, farm ponds, and a pair of Department of Game and Inland Fisheries lakes, both old millponds, Chandler's Millpond and Gardy's Millpond.

Largemouth bass, bluegills, black crappie, channel catfish, both chain and redfin pickerel, pumpkinseed, flier, warmouth, and redbreast and redear sunfish are typical of the freshwater fish found in this region. The variety is rich. During the spring river herring make spawning runs up some of the streams, including the one that feeds Gardy's Millpond. Many of these fish are found in farm ponds, the department lakes, and coves of the Potomac and Rappahannock Rivers. Shad, striped bass, and yellow and white perch also make spawning runs up the two big rivers.

CHANDLER'S MILLPOND

SUPERVISING OFFICE: Department of Game and Inland Fisheries, 5806 Mooretown Road, Williamsburg, VA 23188. Telephone (757) 253-7072

LOCATION: Westmoreland County

SIZE: 75 acres

DIRECTIONS: Virginia Primary Route 3 crosses the lake just west of Montross. Going west, the dam is on the left, and the reverse going east. The access point and boat-launching ramp are just off the highway to the north, or upstream, immediately after you cross the millpond headed west—or just before you enter the bridge going east.

Chandler's Millpond is part of the rich history of the Northern Neck. It was built at least 300 years ago to provide waterpower for Chandler's Grist Mill, which operated through most of the 1940s. It was the oldest gristmill in Westmoreland County, and Chandler's Millpond is the oldest millpond in the county, and certainly among the oldest in Virginia. Thomas Newton acquired the millpond and the mill in the 1700s, rebuilt the mill, and enlarged the dam. Unusually heavy rains breached the dam of the impoundment in September 1992, but the Department of Game and Inland Fisheries has since acquired the property, and the agency rebuilt the dam and installed an emergency spillway to handle heavy flows of water during future storms. The department also installed a Denil fish ladder to accommodate river herring, which historically have made spring spawning runs up the stream that forms the millpond.

The present fishing lake is a joint effort of the Department of Game and Inland Fisheries, the Westmoreland County Board of Supervisors, and the American Legion Post 252.

Typical of flat-country impoundments, the lake is relatively shallow, averaging only 4 feet in depth. It, however, is a rich fishing lake with an abundance of aquatic vegetation. Fallen trees are scattered along the shoreline, providing additional good fish habitat, good spots for locating schooling crappie during the spring months. The surrounding shore is mostly forested with mixed pine and hardwood forests. Across from the launching area is a broad peninsula between the two prongs that form the lake. Generally the surrounding countryside slopes gently to the water's edge. The peninsula is mostly open grassland with a dwelling high on a hill well back from the lake. There are other dwellings around the millpond, but they are well back from the water. The department owns the first 50 feet all around the lake. A small portion of the lake is immediately downstream from the Route 3 bridge, but there is ample space beneath the bridge for boats to pass to the lower water just behind the dam. There is a small pier on the lake near the dam, but it is private and not available for public use. Normally private piers are not allowed on these lakes, but a grandfather clause protects a few of them.

The concrete launching ramp is moderately steep but easy to approach. There is ample parking space overlooking the lake, and directly across the lake is the American Legion meeting hall. Also adjacent to the launching area are a recreational area and a ballpark. A courtesy pier extending out over the lake completes the access point facilities. There is also good bank fishing for those who do not own a boat or prefer not to fish from one.

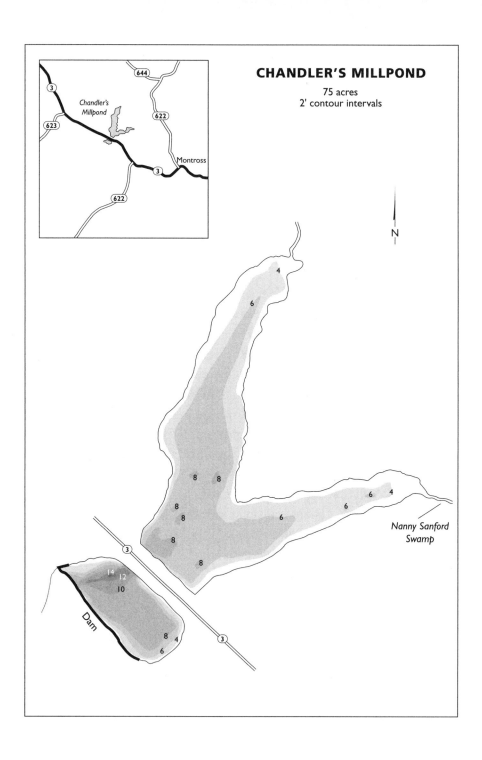

CHANDLER'S MILLPOND

75 acres
2' contour intervals

Nanny Sanford
Swamp

Dam

The fish population is varied and rich, offering species found in few other Virginia waters. Chandler's Millpond is located in prime largemouth bass–fishing country. The aquatic vegetation in the water favors the popular fish, but a survey conducted by department biologists in 1996–97 showed that bass were not as abundant as they should be. As a result, the department has temporarily imposed catch-and-release bass-fishing restrictions. In other words, fishing for bass is currently permitted, but all fish must be released. How long this restriction will remain in effect is not yet known.

Following the rebuilding of the dam after the 1992 breaching, the lake was restocked with bluegills, channel catfish, largemouth bass, and redear sunfish, better known as shellcrackers.

In addition to the species stocked, fish native to the waters include black crappie, pumpkinseed, fliers, redbreast sunfish, and redfin pickerel. Neither the flier nor redfin pickerel is abundant in Virginia, and this millpond provides anglers a chance to catch these interesting fish. The flier, sometimes called the round sunfish, is a member of the sunfish family, and the redfin pickerel is a member of the chain pickerel and grass pickerel family. The chain is by far the largest and the most popular of the pickerels in Virginia and is found in many Virginia waters. The redfin and grass are much smaller, rarely exceeding a foot in length. They are often called the little pickerels. The redfin is found in the far eastern part of the state, and a few grass pickerel inhabit some far western waters.

No gasoline motors or sailboats are allowed on this millpond, but electric motors are permitted. Swimming is also prohibited. Canoes and small boats propelled by oars or paddles are allowed, however, and launching a canoe and paddling quietly along the timbered shoreline watching for birds and other wildlife can be a delightful way to spend a few hours. There are many small coves to explore, or maybe going ashore at a delightful spot for a picnic might be appealing. Other users of the lake, however, should keep in mind that this lake was acquired with funds generated by anglers' license and tax money. They paid for it, and consideration should be given them when canoeing or boating.

The angler launching his boat at the access point has three options. He can turn right, go under the bridge, and fish the deeper water behind the dam; go across the lake and take the eastern prong, which forms in Nanny Sanford Swamp; or turn left and fish the larger and longer western prong.

GARDY'S MILLPOND

SUPERVISING OFFICE: Department of Game and Inland Fisheries, 5806 Mooretown Road, Williamsburg, VA 23188. Telephone (757) 253-7072

LOCATION: Northumberland and Westmoreland Counties

SIZE: 75 acres

DIRECTIONS: From Callao go north on Virginia Primary Route 202 approximately 3 miles and turn left on Virginia Primary Route 617, Gardy's Mill Road, which crosses the Gardy's Millpond dam. There are actually two Route 617s, but driving from the south on Route 202 you take the second one, the one called Gardy's Mill Road. From the north it will be the first one. Route 617 crosses the dam and at the north end of the dam turns left into the parking area and boat-launching ramp. From the north, turn right on Route 617.

Gardy's Millpond, like its twin, 75-acre Chandler's Millpond, once served a water-operated gristmill. It is located in a tranquil setting along the Northumberland-Westmoreland Counties border hard on the broad Potomac River. It is one of the easiest lakes in the state to access, the parking area and launching ramp being just off Virginia Primary Route 617, which crosses the dam. To the left as the road enters the dam, there is a residence and across the road the remains of an old mill, obviously once operated by waterpower from the impoundment. You can stand on the low dam and get a good idea of how shallow the lake is as it spreads over a wide area of the flat Northern Neck country. Gardy's Millpond has also suffered from storm damage and flooding over the years. When Hurricane Bob hit Virginia in 1985, it flooded the Northern Neck region and breached the dam holding back the old millpond, and the lake disappeared. Under the direction of the Department of Game and Inland Fisheries, however, a new dam was constructed, and a spillway was installed to handle future floods. Upon the completion of the new dam and the restoration of the lake, it was stocked with a variety of fish and opened to the public in 1990.

The lake is now the property of the Department of Game and Inland Fisheries—and the anglers of Virginia.

Gardy's Millpond is located in flat country, and the water is relatively shallow, averaging only 5 feet, generally a bit deeper than Chandler's Millpond. Strong growths of aquatic vegetation offer excellent cover for a rich variety of warmwater fish, and the shoreline is dotted with rotting fallen trees that attract spawning crappie and other popular fish. The shoreline is generally forested with a rich mixture of hardwoods and pine. The upper reaches of the lake are shallow and swampy. The department owns 50 feet of shore all around the lake, though at least one dwelling encroaches on that public property. Fishing from the shore is possible just about all around the lake, except at the lakeside dwelling on the left as you approach the lake on Gardy's Mill Road. This is private property, and the yard extends to the lake and is off-limits except by permission from the landowner. Two deep prongs give the lake its character. The mouth of one is immediately across the lake from the launching ramp. This prong extends far south. The launching ramp is on the main prong of the lake, which extends westward.

The concrete launching ramp is short with a very modest grade. There is also a courtesy pier where you can tie your boat while parking your towing vehicle. Actually cartop boats are popular on this calm and shallow lake.

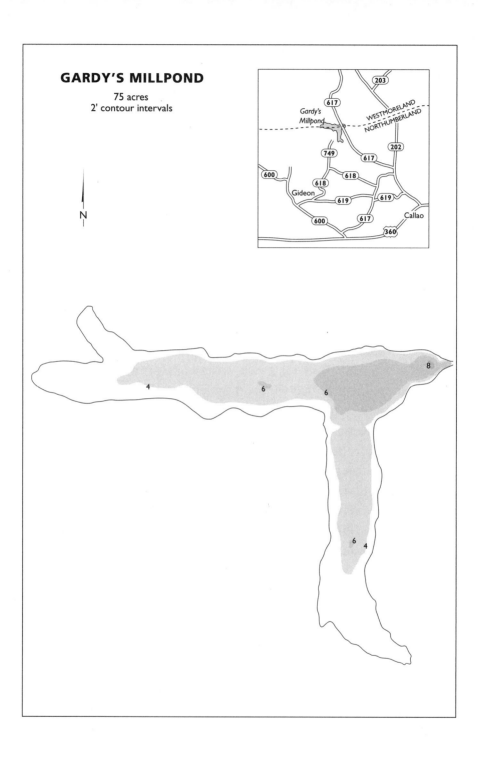

GARDY'S MILLPOND

75 acres
2' contour intervals

N

Gardy's
Millpond

WESTMORELAND
NORTHUMBERLAND

203
617
617
202
749
600
618
618
619
619
Gideon
600
617
Callao
360

4

6

6

8

6 4

The fish population is rich, offering a great variety of the more popular species of warmwater game fish. Largemouth bass, bluegills, and crappie are probably the most popular, but there are also strong populations of channel catfish and chain pickerel. Surveys indicate that many of the bluegills exceed 8 inches in length, a good bluegill in any water. The crappie are the black crappie strain as opposed to the white crappies more common in much of Virginia. There are also good populations of redear sunfish, probably more popularly known as shellcrackers. Populations of pumpkinseed and warmouth are also present.

Those who do not fish but enjoy nature or bird-watching can launch a light canoe and cruise the shoreline alert for a variety of birds, mammals, or other forms of wildlife, turtles, for example. Just enjoying the rich autumn foliage is a possibility in October or early November. Winter comes later to this part of the state than it does in the mountains to the west.

The angler launching his boat at the boat ramp has a pair of options. He can go straight across the lake and fish the deep cove running into the woodlands to the south or swing right and go up the main body of the lake. One good approach might to be to run up the lake to its headwaters and fish one of the shorelines back to the launching ramp, one of a number of options available to anglers on this picturesque lake in the Northern Neck.

THE COUNTIES OF Alleghany, Augusta, Bath, Botetourt, Clark,
   Frederick, Highland, Page, Rockbridge, Rockingham,
   Shenandoah, and Warren

This is a region of rugged mountains, the Alleghenies and the Blue Ridge, and the rich Shenandoah Valley, sparkling trout streams, and rushing rivers. It stretches west from the Blue Ridge Mountains to the West Virginia border and north from Roanoke also to the West Virginia line. Fishermen here are drawn mostly to the fast-flowing rivers such as the Cowpasture and Jackson, which join at Iron Gate to form the James; the upper James; the Maury, which skirts Lexington; the Middle, North, and South Rivers, which join to form the South Fork of the Shenandoah; and the North Fork of the Shenandoah, which joins the South Fork at Front Royal to form the main stem. All are prime smallmouth bass streams. Equally as popular are the hundreds of trout streams that race down the western slope of the Blue Ridge Mountains and lace the rugged Allegheny Mountains to the west. They offer fishing for native brook trout and wild populations of introduced browns and rainbows. Dozens of put-and-take trout streams, where hatchery trout are stocked regularly through all but the hottest months of the year, are the choice of many anglers. There are scattered small ponds throughout much of the George Washington and Jefferson National Forests, but the major and only big water in this land of mountains and valleys is Lake Moomaw on the Jackson River north of Covington. It is noted for its big brown trout and rainbow trout but also offers good yellow perch fishing and largemouth bass. A trio of Department of Game and Inland Fisheries lakes, A. Willis Robertson, Frederick, and Shenandoah, offer well-managed fishing water. We look more closely at those interesting waters here.

While smallmouth bass and brook, brown, and rainbow trout are the major fishing attraction in this area, there are also largemouth bass, bluegills, black and white crappie, bullhead and channel catfish, chain pickerel, muskellunge, pumpkinseed, redbreast and redear sunfish, walleyes, and warmouth. The variety of fish is rich in this spectacular land.

LAKE A. WILLIS ROBERTSON

SUPERVISING OFFICE: Department of Game and Inland Fisheries, P.O. Box 996, Verona, VA 24482. Telephone (540) 248-9360

LOCATION: Rockbridge County

SIZE: 31 acres

DIRECTIONS: Take exit 55 south off Interstate 64 and follow U.S. Highway 11 south to Lexington, and then U.S. Highway 11 South Bypass to the first stoplight. A brown sign there points straight ahead to the lake. Pick up Virginia Primary Route 251 at the stoplight and follow the brown signs. Some say "Public Fishing Lake," but others say "Lake A. Willis Robertson." Cross Buffalo Creek and turn right. You will follow Buffalo Creek much of the way but watch for the signs. The lake is approximately 14 miles southwest of Lexington.

Lake Robertson is the center of an outdoor recreation complex operated by Rockbridge County on 75 acres leased from the Department of Game and Inland Fisheries. It is part of a 581-acre tract owned by the department and managed pri-

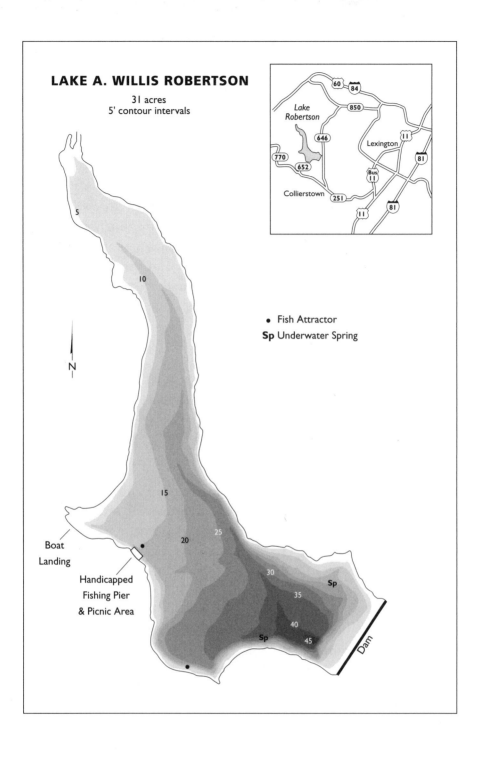

LAKE A. WILLIS ROBERTSON

31 acres
5' contour intervals

Lake
Robertson

60 84
850
646
770
652
Lexington 11
81
Bus 11

Collierstown 251
11 81

• Fish Attractor
Sp Underwater Spring

N

5

10

15

20
25

Boat
Landing

Handicapped
Fishing Pier
& Picnic Area

30
35
Sp

40
45
Sp

Dam

marily for hunting and fishing. As is true of all of the department lakes, swimming is prohibited. It is located on the eastern slopes of the Allegheny Mountains and adjoins the George Washington and Jefferson National Forests. Other than fishing, about the only water recreation permitted is canoeing or other forms of boating. Gasoline motors are not allowed, and this eliminates water skiing. Electric motors are permitted as they are on most department lakes.

Built in 1971 as a joint project of the Department of Game and Inland Fisheries, Rockbridge County, the Virginia Department of Parks and Recreation, the Virginia Commission of Outdoor Recreation, and the U.S. Department of the Interior, the lake was named for the late U.S. senator A. Willis Robertson, also the first chairman of the Virginia Department of Game and Inland Fisheries. The senator was an ardent angler and hunter and an early proponent of modern game and fisheries management and natural resources conservation.

At the lake are a developed fifty-three-site campground, a roomy picnic shelter, and other recreational facilities. And many attractive hiking trails. All sites have a fire ring, picnic table, and electrical and water hookups. A hiking trail circles the lake with several bridges crossing small streams or arms of the lake. Additionally there are many other trails that lead the hiker throughout the area. They range in length from a half mile to a mile and a half. It is a popular spot for family outings, with plenty of parking space for automobiles. There is also a concession with an attendant on duty to provide information and answer questions. While the lake is open to fishing 24 hours a day, the other facilities are limited to normal daylight hours. Additional recreational facilities include a swimming pool and bathhouse, comfort stations with individual showers and dressing rooms, a tennis court, and volleyball, badminton, and softball fields. The picnic ground includes fireplaces and tables, and there is a group picnic shelter with two fireplaces, tables, and restrooms. The shelter will accommodate up to 150 people.

This is an ideal lake for an angler to take his family where he can fish while the family enjoys the other facilities.

Amid all of this activity the fisherman can enjoy good fishing in a relatively undisturbed atmosphere. The department officials have seen to that. Midway between the dam and the upper reaches of the lake are a boat-launching ramp and parking space for automobiles and boat trailers. A floating boat dock and a courtesy pier are also located there. Rental boats are locked, but the keys are available at the office near the entrance. There are also oars or paddles and life preservers, all for rent at a modest fee. A handicapped fishing pier and picnic area are located between the boat-launching area and dam. And nearby is a fish-cleaning station, something not found on many of the department lakes.

The lake is noted for an abundance of bluegills with many in the 6-to-8-inch range. Look for the lunker bluegills near beaver lodges and brush during early spring. Some big largemouth bass dwell in the lake, but they can be difficult to catch. There are also good populations of bullhead and channel catfish—channels up to 25 pounds or more. Other panfish include pumpkinseed, warmouth, and both redbreast and redear sunfish. Walleyes have been stocked.

Depths range from 5 feet or less in the upper reaches to 45 feet or more near the dam, but the average depth is 18 feet. The lake is located in the mountainous country of western Rockbridge County, and the water is crystal clear, presenting a true challenge to anglers. The visibility is excellent, and the bass tend to shy off when approached during the fall and spring when they cruise in the shallows. The clear water allows the sun to penetrate and encourage the growth of pondweed and other vegetation. Grass carp have been introduced to control these plants. Old roadbeds, structures of various kinds, and numerous springs cover much of the bottom. Weed beds and openings in the weed beds are good places to look for big bass and jumbo bluegills. Fish attractors made of cedar are also good places to look for these two popular fish.

A. Willis Robertson can be a challenging lake to fish, but it can be productive for those who learn its secrets.

LAKE FREDERICK

SUPERVISING OFFICE: Department of Game and Inland Fisheries, P.O. Box 996, Verona, VA 24482. Telephone (540) 248-9360

LOCATION: Frederick County

SIZE: 117 acres

DIRECTIONS: The lake is located just off U.S. Highway 340 approximately 6 miles north of Front Royal. Watch for brown signs for "Public Fishing Lake." Turn left if going north on Route 340 and right if driving south. The lake is a short distance to the west from Route 340. Very easy to locate. A paved road leads from Route 340 directly to the lake.

Developed by the Department of Game and Inland Fisheries and opened to fishing in 1990, this is a beautiful lake, for the most part surrounded by mixed pine and hardwood forests. The shoreline is undeveloped, but this may be temporary. It is the northernmost public fishing lake in Virginia and convenient to the densely populated Northern Virginia region. It is also the largest public fishing lake in the Shenandoah Valley.

Depths range from less than 8 feet in the back of some of the coves to approximately 55 feet in the deep water behind the dam. This wide range of deep and shallow water offers a rich variety of fishing opportunities—and challenges. In the upper reaches and in some of the smaller coves, there is a good deal of dead standing timber that was left when the area was flooded. This provides excellent cover for a variety of fish as well as interesting challenges for the angler.

The lake is made up primarily of a pair of deep coves that stretch north from the boat-launching ramp. Looking north from the ramp, the longer one is on the left. The shorter one,

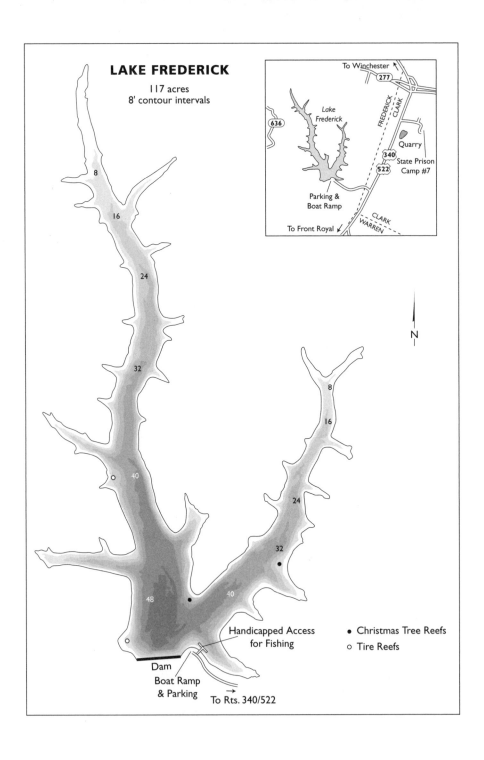

LAKE FREDERICK

117 acres
8' contour intervals

To Winchester
277
636
Lake
Frederick
FREDERICK
CLARK
Quarry
340
State Prison
522
Camp #7
Parking &
Boat Ramp
To Front Royal
CLARK
WARREN

8

16

24

32

40

8

16

24

32

48

40

N

Handicapped Access
for Fishing

• Christmas Tree Reefs
○ Tire Reefs

Dam

Boat Ramp
& Parking

To Rts. 340/522

approximately half the length of the longer one, stretches away to the right. Numerous other smaller coves and points offer fishing opportunities for anglers who know how to read lake water.

Generally the lake banks pitch quickly to deep water, but the water is clear much of the year, allowing the sun to reach the bottom in shallow areas. This encourages the growth of aquatic vegetation and cover for small fish.

A pair of large reefs of 100 Christmas trees each were installed in February 1996 soon after 1995 Christmas trees had been discarded. Smaller such reefs have been placed at other points in the lake. There is a handicapped fishing pier near the boat-launching area, and a brush reef is maintained around it. There is also an automobile tire reef near the far end of the dam. These reefs are appropriately marked with buoys.

In addition to the handicapped fishing pier, this lake has a concrete boat-launching ramp, a floating courtesy pier, and a roomy parking lot for automobiles and trailers. Rental johnboats with electric motors and batteries are available at the concession stand near the launching ramp. The concession stand offers limited fishing tackle, including a wide variety of baits proven successful in the lake. While the lake is open to fishing 24 hours a day, the concession is open only during hours of daylight.

There is good bank fishing in the vicinity of the boat-launching ramp and concession stand, and you can fish from the dam.

The fish population is rich and mixed, offering a good choice of angling opportunities. Largemouth bass, black crappie, channel catfish, redear sunfish, and walleyes are the major species, though northern pike have been introduced, adding to an already interesting variety. Largemouth, protected by a slot limit, grow to trophy size, and the bluegills and redear sunfish are of good size. So are the black crappie. Channel catfish up to 24 pounds have been caught. Creel and size limits are posted near the boat-launching ramp. Check them carefully.

Lake Frederick is a beautiful body of water that offers good fishing in a spectacular setting.

LAKE SHENANDOAH

SUPERVISING OFFICE: Department of Game and Inland Fisheries, P.O. Box 996, Verona, VA 24482. Telephone (540) 248-9360

LOCATION: Rockingham County

SIZE: 36 acres

DIRECTIONS: Secondary Route 689 off U.S. Highway 33 just east of Harrisonburg leads directly to the lake. Approximately 2 miles. From the east turn left on Route 689, or from the west turn right. Look for a sign at the highway. A short distance from Route 33 there is a stop sign; stop and then proceed straight ahead to the entrance to the lake.

Lake Shenandoah was built by the Department of Game and Inland Fisheries in 1957 to become a put-and-take trout lake. It was quickly discovered that the lake was more appropriate for warmwater fish, and it was stocked with bass, bluegills, and other fish that prospered. The stocking of trout was then eventually discontinued. Located in a large basin easily accessible from Route 33 between Elkton and Harrisonburg, the lake offers good fishing for warmwater species. It's approximately 2 miles off Route 33. The area around the lake is rapidly developing into a suburban residential area, and runoff from heavily fertilized lawns and a nearby golf course could eventually affect the fishing. Fertilization is good for any fishing water—unless the water eventually suffers from overenrichment. Currently under consideration is a plan to dredge the two arms of the lake and hopefully create a wetland which will capture much of the sediment runoff. A local organization called the Lake Shenandoah Preservation Association keeps an eye on the lake. Among other things the association has fenced much of

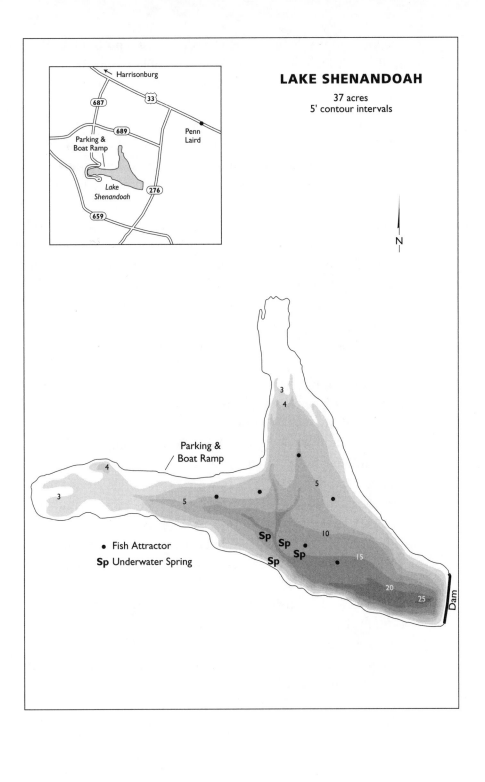

LAKE SHENANDOAH

37 acres
5' contour intervals

Harrisonburg

687
33

689

Penn
Laird

Parking &
Boat Ramp

276

Lake
Shenandoah

659

N

3
4

Parking &
Boat Ramp

4

3

5

5

• Fish Attractor
Sp Underwater Spring

Sp Sp
Sp
Sp Sp

10

15

20
25

Dam

the area from vehicular use, reseeded grass, and built a hiking trail which includes a wheelchair-accessible footbridge over an uplake arm of the lake. Benches have been located along the lakeshore for picnicking or relaxing.

Springs in the lake maintain healthy levels of water. The lake is located in a large basin with two arms that extend north and west from the launching area. Weeds and willows line much of the shoreline. The water is shallow, 3 feet or less in the upper reaches of the two arms to 25 feet or more behind the dam. Much of the water, however, is 5 feet or less in depth. The shoreline vegetation is mostly limited to grass and weeds except for the southern shoreline of the main basin where the banks are steep and wooded with overhanging trees and rock slabs. Facilities are limited but adequate. The concrete boat-launching ramp provides quick and easy access to the lake, and a courtesy pier provides a place for anglers to tie up their boats while driving their towing vehicles and boat trailers to the roomy gravel parking lot—or while retrieving them at the end of trip. The walking trail that circles the entire lake offers good bank fishing. There was once a concession stand on the lake near the launching area, but it has long since been closed. The building, however, still stands.

The fish population is rich, with muskellunge adding an interesting dimension to the usual warmwater fish population. Some of the big fish have grown to trophy size, but a big muskie is hard to catch—as in any water it fins. The largemouth bass grow to trophy size under restricted creel and size limits. Other fish include black crappie, bluegills, carp, channel catfish, and pumpkinseed sunfish. The crappie and sunfish are abundant, though they tend to run small. Catfish up to 15 pounds have been reported. Carp are also abundant—and big.

The country around this 37-acre lake is grassy and open, typical of the beautiful Shenandoah Valley.

THE COUNTIES OF Amelia, Appomattox, Bedford, Brunswick,
   Buckingham, Campbell, Charlotte, Chesterfield, Cumberland,
   Franklin, Dinwiddie, Greensville, Halifax, Henry, Isle of Wight,
   Lunenburg, Mecklenburg, Nottoway, Patrick, Pittsylvania,
   Powhatan, Prince Edward, Prince George, Surry, and Sussex

Southside Virginia is rich farming county. Tobacco is big here, and to the east in the Suffolk area, peanuts are king, for this is "the peanut capital of the world." But like much of Virginia, the region is changing. Tobacco farmers are struggling to keep alive a once productive way of life, and family farms are being sold to timber companies that plant them in fast-growing loblolly pines. Once-rich hardwoods are slowly disappearing in favor of the economically more productive pines. Family farms, once the very heart of this rich farming country, are slowly disappearing and with them a rich way of life. Fields that under crop rotation were planted in alternate years in corn, hay, and wheat are now being converted to grasslands and cattle raising.

This unique part of Virginia lies generally south of the James River, stretching south to the North Carolina line, west to the Blue Ridge Mountains, and east to tidewater and the Atlantic coast.

For generations this was small-game hunting country with an abundance of rabbits and squirrels. The bobwhite quail was king. The loblolly pines that have replaced hardwood forests have reduced the squirrel populations, and the fading of crop farming has eliminated much of the prime habitat that supported quail and rabbits. Now there is a thriving whitetail deer population which barely existed a half century ago. And wild turkeys have made a dramatic comeback.

The proliferation of farm ponds and the coming of big reservoirs such as Buggs Island Lake have brought a new kind of fishing to Southside Virginia. Other large lakes or impoundments include Smith Mountain Lake and Philpott Lake in the western part of the region. To the east there is Chesdin Reservoir near Petersburg. For generations the primary fishing was in rivers and streams, often badly colored from runoff of rainwater from agricultural operations. There is still good stream fishing here beginning with the James River to the north and including the Dan and Roanoke/Staunton Rivers along the North Carolina border. The Appomattox River rises in the Farmville area and flows east to enter the James River near Petersburg. The Blackwater, Meherrin, and Nottoway Rivers flow south into North Carolina.

Still-water fishing, however, has been enhanced by the Department of Game and Inland Fisheries system of public fishing lakes. There are more such waters in Southside Virginia than in any other part of the state. There are almost a dozen such lakes and ponds in this sprawling region. The largest lakes in the department's system are also found here.

Largemouth bass, bluegills, crappies, and shellcrackers, or redear sunfish, dominate the fishing in these warmest waters in the state. Also finning these fertile waters are both black and white crappie, bullhead, channel and white catfish, chain pickerel, walleye, and yellow perch.

LAKE AIRFIELD

SUPERVISING OFFICE: Department of Game and Inland Fisheries, Deep Creek, 3909 Airline Boulevard, Chesapeake, VA 23321. Telephone (757) 465-6811

LOCATION: Sussex County

SIZE: 105 acres

DIRECTIONS: U.S. Highway 460 at Wakefield is the turnoff point to Lake Airfield. Secondary Route 628 to the south leads to the lake. There is a stoplight on Route 460 in Wakefield where a brown sign reading "Public Fishing Lake" points the way. There is also a brown sign pointing in the direction of the Lake Airfield 4-H Center. From the west on Route 460, turn right on Route 628, and from the east turn left. The distance to the lake from Route 460 is short. A sign on the right points to the 4-H center, but continue past this sign, and the lake will appear through the trees to the right. Cross a small bridge over the stream draining the lake, and the launching ramp will be on the right—just off Route 628.

Airfield is a unique and productive fishing lake hosting a great variety of fish in water rich in aquatic vegetation. Milfoil covers much of the lake during the summer months, which can be hot and humid in this part of Virginia. The shoreline is rich in vegetation such as pickerel weed, water lilies, and water shield, providing rich cover for a great variety of fish. The lake is surrounded by forests of mixed hardwoods and pine and several swamps. There is a good deal of standing timber in some of the coves. This is a shallow lake averaging only 6 feet in depth with maximum depths in the 10- to 12-foot range. The water is stained as is typical of waters in this part of Virginia, "black water" but otherwise clear.

Directly across the lake from the boat-launching ramp, the Lake Airfield 4-H Center occupies much of a broad point that extends into the lake. A deep cove running up one side of the point is filled with standing timber, much of it cypress trees. Swimming is not permitted in the lake, but visiting campers might roam the lake in 4-H Center canoes. Gasoline outboard motors are also prohibited, but electric motors are permitted. Propelled by a fully charged marine battery, they provide easy access to the lake. Fishing hours are an hour before sunrise until an hour after sunset, but this could be changed as most de-

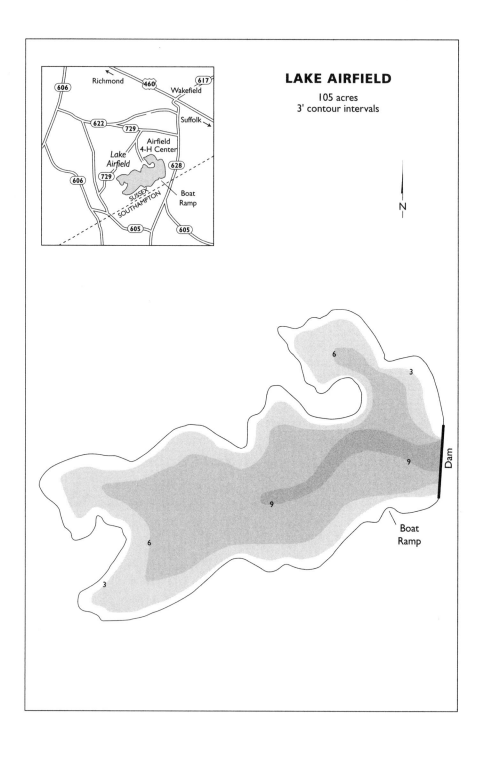

LAKE AIRFIELD

105 acres
3' contour intervals

Richmond

606
460
617
Wakefield

Suffolk

622
729

Airfield
4-H Center

Lake
Airfield

628

606
729

Boat
Ramp

SUSSEX
SOUTHAMPTON

605
605

N

6

3

9

Dam

9

6

Boat
Ramp

3

partment lakes are open to fishing 24 hours a day. Check the regulations posted near the launching ramp before embarking on a fishing trip.

Impounded in 1947, the lake has never been overly popular, probably because of the abundance of good freshwater fishing in the area, the nearby and popular Suffolk Lakes, for example.

The facilities are adequate, though not spectacular. There is a boat-launching ramp near the dam as well as a courtesy pier intended primarily for tying up a boat while it is being loaded and while parking the towing vehicle and boat trailer. Parking space is not spacious but adequate for parking a dozen automobiles and boat trailers. There is also a restroom at the boat-launching area.

The fish population is rich, including largemouth bass, black crappie, bluegills, chain pickerel, yellow bullheads, and yellow perch. Compared to other waters in southeastern Virginia, the fish here tend to run large, though not abundant. Experienced anglers feel the bass fishing is best in early spring and early fall.

A few hours spent fishing the dark waters of this quiet, somewhat secluded lake can be a rewarding angling experience. And stop in Wakefield and pick up some of its famous peanuts on your way home.

Sailboats and swimming are prohibited, but those who do not fish might enjoy launching a canoe and cruising the shoreline alert for songbirds and other wildlife that inhabits the area.

LAKE AMELIA

SUPERVISING OFFICE: Department of Game and Inland Fisheries, HC 6, Box 46, Farmville, VA 23901. Telephone (434) 392-9645

LOCATION: Amelia County

SIZE: 100 acres

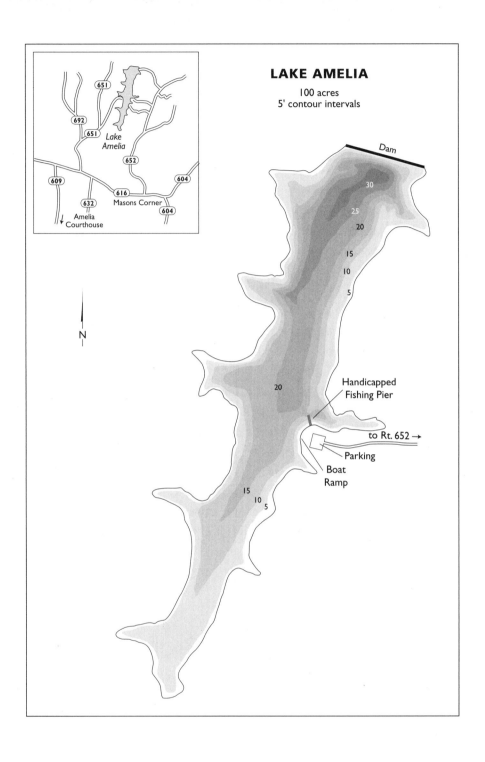

LAKE AMELIA

100 acres
5' contour intervals

651

692

651 *Lake Amelia*

652

609

616

604

632

604

Masons Corner

Amelia
Courthouse

N

Dam

30

25

20

15

10

5

20

Handicapped
Fishing Pier

to Rt. 652 →

Parking

Boat
Ramp

15

10

5

DIRECTIONS: The lake is within the Amelia Wildlife Management Area south of U.S. Highway 60 and north of U.S. Highway 360. From Highway 60, go south on Virginia Primary Highway 13 to Secondary Route 609 and left on Route 616 to the wildlife management area sign on left. Take the road leading into area, turn left at the sign for "Public Boat Ramp," and follow the road to the lake. From U.S. Highway 360, approximately 5 miles east of Amelia Courthouse, take Secondary Route 604 north to Route 616. A wildlife management area sign on Route 604 indicates the turn. Follow Route 616 west to the wildlife management area sign on the right and then follow the directions as given above.

Lake Amelia is located within the 2,217-acre Amelia Wildlife Management Area, an area managed by the Department of Game and Inland Fisheries for wildlife and public hunting. The fishing facilities are excellent, including a spacious concrete boat-launching ramp and a carpeted fishing pier. A paved walk leads from the parking area to the fishing pier, which accommodates handicapped anglers. There is also a courtesy pier at the boat dock where launched boats can be tied up for loading or unloading.

Constructed by the Department of Game and Inland Fisheries, this is a beautiful lake surrounded by mixed pine and hardwood forests in gently rolling piedmont country. It is a relatively deep lake averaging 16 feet in depth, but the water behind the dam runs up to depths of 30 feet. The stream that forms the lake drains into the nearby Appomattox River. There are a number of coves, some shallow ones but others that probe deeply into the countryside. One of the deepest ones is on the right immediately down the lake from the launching ramp. The coves and points offer opportunities for anglers who have learned to read a lake.

The attractive lake is convenient to anglers in the densely populated Richmond area. Being in a publicly owned wildlife management area, it is protected from development. Other facilities include Porta-Jon restrooms in the vicinity of the launching ramp. Sailboats and swimming are prohibited, but those who do not fish might enjoy launching a canoe and cruising the shoreline watching for songbirds and other wildlife.

The upper reaches of the lake are relatively shallow, with much of the water 5 feet or less deep. It can be a challenging lake to fish. Trees along the shoreline, left in the lake when it was impounded, have now rotted and fallen into the water, providing good fish habitat. Shoreline vegetation and aquatic vegetation also provide good cover and shallow-water fishing for those who like to work a shoreline.

The fish population is rich and varied. Present are largemouth bass, black crappie, bluegills, channel catfish, redear sunfish, or shellcrackers, and walleyes. Channel catfish are stocked every two years, but the walleyes are stocked annually. The deep water near the dam appeals to the walleye, a fish that shuns sunlight. They are best fished for in the deepest part of the lake near the dam. Largemouth bass are particularly abundant and average 1 to 2 pounds. The sunfish, the bluegills and redear sunfish, are also abundant and average a half pound.

As is true of most department lakes, gasoline outboard motors are prohibited, but electric motors are permitted. Fishing hours are normally an hour before sunrise until an hour after sunset. The current regulations are posted near the boat ramp, however, and may be changed from time to time. Check them for size and creel limits.

This is a picturesque lake and a joy to be on.

BRIERY CREEK LAKE

SUPERVISING OFFICE: Department of Game and Inland Fisheries, HC 6, Box 46, Farmville, VA 23901. Telephone (434) 392-9645

LOCATION: Prince Edward County

SIZE: 845 acres

DIRECTIONS: The lake is located 7 miles south of Farmville on U.S. Highway 15, and the dam is visible from the highway. There are two boat-launching areas, one near the dam and the other near the headwaters of the lake. The one near the dam is just south of the turnoff to Hampden-Sydney College. Briery Creek Road, just north of the dam, leads to a pair of lower lake ramps. There is a "Public Boat Landing" sign on U.S. Highway 15 on the west side of the highway. From the north, turn right into this access road, and from the south turn left. The first launching area on the left features a concrete boat-launching ramp, a courtesy pier, a paved parking lot for automobiles and boat trailers, and a restroom. A short distance up the lake, also on the left, is a gravel launching ramp, a handicapped-accessible fishing pier, and another restroom. Several miles south of the dam, Secondary Route 701 leads west off U.S. Highway 15 to the boat-launching ramp on the upper reaches of the lake. A "Public Boat Landing" sign on the west side of the highway points to the launching area. This area also features a concrete boat-launching ramp, ample parking space for automobiles and boat trailers, and a restroom. There are also several bank-fishing areas where a light hand-carried boat can be launched. Both are on the west side of the lake, one at the end of Secondary Route 705 and the other at the end of Secondary Route 701.

Briery Creek Lake, an impoundment on Briery Creek, at 845 acres is the largest of the thirty-two Department of Game and Inland Fisheries lakes. It is also one of the few where gasoline outboard motors of 10 horsepower or less are permitted. It is well to bear in mind, however, that much of the standing timber was left in the lake when it was impounded, and outboard motor operators should be aware of possible underwater timber, stumps, and other obstructions that can damage a motor propeller. The slowly decaying timber provides excellent cover for the fish but can challenge the angler, who risks frequent hang-ups. The lake is located within the 3,164-acre Briery Creek

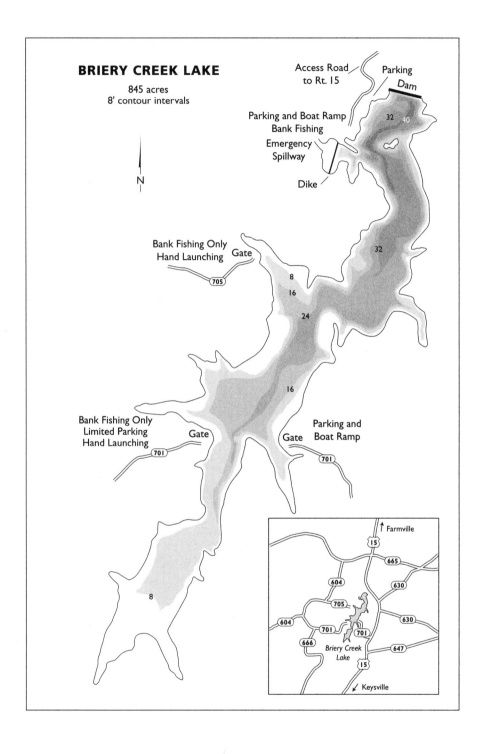

BRIERY CREEK LAKE

845 acres
8' contour intervals

N

Access Road
to Rt. 15

Parking

Dam

Parking and Boat Ramp
Bank Fishing

32   40

Emergency
Spillway

Dike

32

Bank Fishing Only
Hand Launching   Gate

8

16

24

705

16

Bank Fishing Only
Limited Parking
Hand Launching   Gate

Gate   Parking and
Boat Ramp

701

701

8

Farmville

15

665

604

630

705

604

630

701   701

666

Briery Creek
Lake

647

15

Keysville

Wildlife Management Area and attracts good numbers of ducks during the fall and winter months. During the late November, December, and January waterfowl season, anglers should expect some competition from duck hunters. This is one of the few department lakes where hunting is allowed. The lake was developed by the Department of Game and Inland Fisheries.

Most of the wildlife management area is covered with mixed hardwood and pine forests, and both deer and turkey hunting are popular, but this does not interfere with fishing. The country is gently rolling, and except for the occasional report of a shotgun during the hunting season, the setting is quiet and peaceful. Nearby on U.S. Highway 15 is a convenience store that serves as an unofficial source of fishing information. It also carries a limited amount of fishing tackle and bait.

The big lake is long and narrow, stretching up the Briery Creek valley from the dam near U.S. Highway 15. The water varies in depth from 8 feet or less to 40 feet behind the dam. There is also a good deal of deep water in the 20- to 30-foot range in the creek channel. Near the shoreline and in the upper reaches of the lake, there is a good bit of shallow-water fishing. There are also a number of coves all around the lake, many of them deep. Just up the lake from the gravel launching area near the dam there is a dike across one of the coves that serves as an emergency spillway. The one small island in the lake is just up from the dam and across from the boat-launching area. In addition to the acres of standing timber that provide good cover for a rich fishing population, a number of small weed beds demand the attention of visiting anglers.

The fish population is rich and varied. Briery Creek holds a good population of chain pickerel. When the lake was first flooded, the fish found ideal habitat and offered exciting fishing for Virginia's member of the pike family. The pickerel fishing is still good, though not as fabulous as it was in the early years of the lake. Once the largemouth bass were introduced, they grew rapidly in the highly favorable environment. The lake became one of the top bass lakes in Virginia, and it consistently gives up lunkers in the 12-pound range. The lunker fishing has declined slightly because of the heavy fishing pressure the lake has been subjected to, but it is still a good bass lake, one of the best. The lake also quickly developed a reputation as a sunfish lake, with both bluegills and redear sunfish in the half-pound range being fairly common. Black crappie and channel catfish were also stocked, and the crappie fishing remains good despite heavy fishing pressure.

Fishing hours are posted at the launching ramps, and the notices should be consulted as this lake is not open 24 hours a day as some are. The standing and rotting timber makes fishing after dark dangerous. Sailboats and swimming are prohibited, but those who do not fish might enjoy launching a canoe and cruising the shoreline alert for songbirds and other wildlife.

LAKE BRUNSWICK

SUPERVISING OFFICE: Department of Game and Inland Fisheries, HC 6, Box 46, Farmville, VA 23901. Telephone (434) 392-9645

LOCATION: Brunswick County

SIZE: 150 acres

DIRECTIONS: The lake is reached by Secondary Route 638 off U.S. Highway 58 approximately 8 miles east of Lawrenceville. The turnoff is actually in the little town of Edgerton. Going east on U.S. Highway 58, the turn is left on Route 638, and headed west it is right. The lake is a short distance from U.S. Highway 58, and Route 638 crosses the lake on a modern bridge. The boat-launching ramp is on the right just before entering the bridge.

At 150 acres Brunswick is one of the largest lakes in the system. It was built by the department in 1955 and is located in gently rolling piedmont country. It is a long, narrow lake with numerous coves and a small island in its lower reaches. There is also a small island down the lake from the boat-launching area. The launching ramp and access point are in the uplake stretch of the attractive body of water. When you drive northeast on Route 638, the ramp is on the right. There is parking on both sides of the road. Just before you get to the modern ramp, there is an old abandoned ramp on the right. While the ramp is no longer in use, the old parking area is still available. Locating a place to park is no problem here. Unlike other department lakes of this size or larger, electric motors only are allowed. No gasoline outboard motors, a typical restriction on the smaller department lakes. Sailboats and swimming are also prohibited.

The concrete launching ramp is modern and just off Route 638 on the right just before the road crosses the lake on a modern bridge. There is also ample parking space for automobiles and boat trailers near the ramp.

The department owns a 20-foot right-of-way around the entire shoreline, providing plenty of opportunities for those who prefer to fish from the banks. A few homes with docks are scattered around the lake, but this does not interfere with bank fishing. Located in a predominantly hardwood forest, the shore is generally surrounded by rich stands of mixed hardwood and pine forests. Because of the proximity of the hardwood forest, the water is slightly stained, as are so many lakes and streams in this part of Virginia. This does not affect the fish or the fishing. Otherwise, the water is generally clear. Aquatic vegetation, mostly along the shoreline, offers good cover for fish and water that anglers like to fish.

While the lake is reasonably shallow, mostly under 10 feet, depths of 15 feet or more are found just behind the dam. Because of its length, trolling is popular among many anglers. There are several large coves north of the Route 638 bridge, and they are relatively shallow. Fishing the shoreline and its rich vegetation should also be productive depending upon the season. Much of the shoreline water is less than 5 feet deep, tempt-

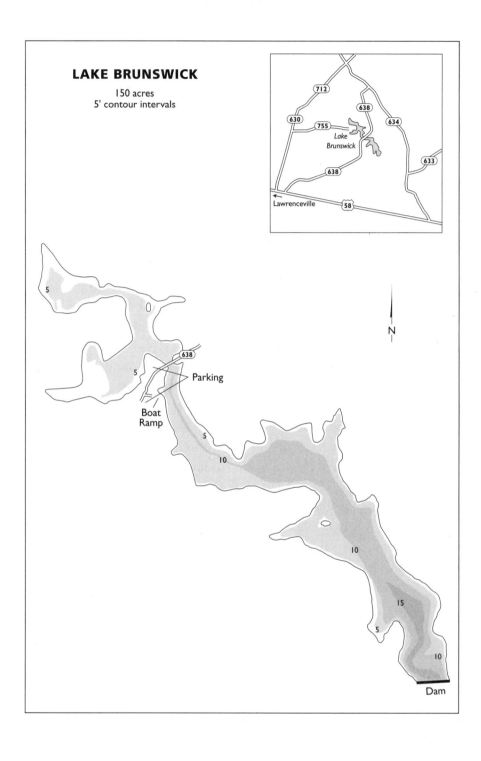

LAKE BRUNSWICK

150 acres
5' contour intervals

712

630

638

755

634

*Lake
Brunswick*

638

633

Lawrenceville

58

5

638

5

Parking

Boat
Ramp

5

10

N

10

15

5

10

Dam

ing for those who like to cast surface lures for bass and chain pickerel.

The fishing is good in Lake Brunswick, and the variety of fish is rich. Largemouth bass are reasonably abundant, with fish in the 8- to 10-pound range to challenge anglers. Black crappie up to 11 inches in length are fairly common, and many blue-gills reach 8 inches. This is chain pickerel country, and the lake offers good fishing for this member of the pike family. Other possibilities include channel catfish, which are stocked by the department; redear sunfish, or shellcrackers; and yellow perch.

Nonanglers might enjoy launching a canoe and paddling along the extensive shoreline alert for birds and other forms of wildlife. Expect to see occasional deer and turkeys.

This is a beautiful upland lake and quickly accessible from U.S. Highway 58.

LAKE BURTON

SUPERVISING OFFICE: Department of Game and Inland Fish-eries, 1132 Thomas Jefferson Road, Forest, VA 24551, (434) 525-7522

LOCATION: Pittsylvania County

SIZE: 76 acres

DIRECTIONS: Take Virginia Primary Highway 57 west out of Chatham on U.S. Highway 29 to Secondary Route 750, Green Pond Road, left on Secondary Route 800, Burton Lake Road, to the lake.

Impounded in 1950, Lake Burton has come of age. It is a beautiful lake located in north-central Pittsylvania County west of Chatham. The country here is the gently rolling west-ern piedmont region. Mixed hardwood and pine forest sur-round much of the lake in a rich farming region. Croplands are extensive. While the Department of Game and Inland Fisher-ies owns 50 feet of land all around the lake, there are scattered

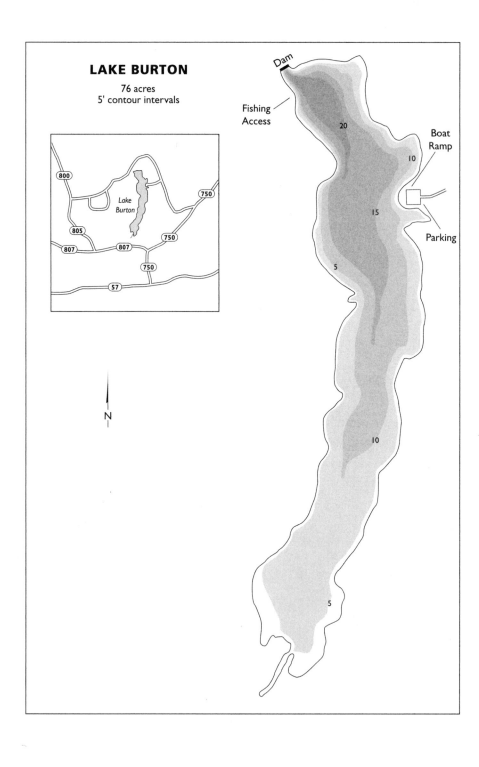

LAKE BURTON

76 acres
5' contour intervals

Lake Burton

800
750
805
750
807
807
750
750
57

N

Dam

Fishing
Access

Boat
Ramp

Parking

20

10

15

5

10

5

residences overlooking the water. In fact, there is one on Route 800 at its junction with the road leading down to the launching ramp.

The lake is long and fairly narrow with relatively undented shoreline. The dam is on the right downlake from the boat-launching ramp. The water is relatively shallow and tends to be infertile, but the department biologists fertilize it periodically, and it supports a good population of game fish as well as forage fish that the bass and other fish feed on. The average depth is approximately 10 feet, but depths range up to 20 feet behind the dam. The water is frequently stained, which actually improves fishing conditions. The upper reaches of the lake are shallow, with much of it measuring 5 feet or less, but it holds an abundance of aquatic vegetation, and there are thick stands of alder along the shoreline. Trees toppled into the lake during storms offer good cover on the southwest shoreline.

The road off Route 800 leads to an excellent concrete boat-launching ramp, and there is somewhat limited but adequate parking space for automobiles and boat trailers. This lake is fairly remote, and the fishing pressure is generally light. The fishing regulations are posted near the launching ramp, and they may vary from time to time. Fishing is permitted 24 hours a day.

The fish population is rich and typical of fishing in this part of Virginia. The largemouth bass fishing is excellent, with the fish enjoying good growth rates. Bass of 6 pounds or more are caught every season. There are good populations of both bullhead and channel catfish, with channel cats running up to 12 pounds. Perhaps unique is the presence of both black and white crappies. Crappies in the 3-pound range are reasonably common. The bluegill fishing, a staple in all of the department lakes, is excellent and supports much of the fishing pressure. Gizzard shad, introduced to the lake, are the major forage fish for bass and other species.

Typically gasoline-powered outboard motors and sailboats

are prohibited. Swimming is also prohibited. Electric outboard motors are allowed and are very popular among anglers. An electric-powered outboard motor on a johnboat is probably the most popular craft on the lake. Nonfishermen might want to launch a light canoe, paddle along the shoreline, and watch for birds and other forms of wildlife or go ashore and find a spot for a picnic lunch. Other users of the lake should keep in mind that anglers' money paid for it so their rights should be respected. In other words, if a pair of anglers is working the shoreline, moving between them and the shore should be avoided.

An angler launching a boat can turn right at the ramp and work toward the dam, turn left and work the eastern shoreline, cross the lake and fish the western shoreline, or take the middle and troll the deeper water. Plenty of options on a beautiful little lake.

LAKE CONNER

SUPERVISING OFFICE: Department of Game and Inland Fisheries, HC 6, Box 46, Farmville, VA 23901. Telephone (434) 392-9645

LOCATION: Halifax County

SIZE: 110 acres

DIRECTIONS: From U.S. 360 east of Halifax, take Secondary Route 746, Mountain Laurel Road, north from Clover to Secondary Route 603, Hunting Creek Road, on the left, then right on Secondary Route 619, Hardings Mill Road, then right on Route 623, Caleo Ferry Road, to Secondary Route 624, Mortons Ferry Road, to the boat-launching ramp. Look for the brown "Boat Launching Ramp" sign at the Route 624 turnoff.

Lake Conner, built in 1954, is located in northern Halifax County in a somewhat remote part of Southside Virginia approximately 20 miles north of South Boston. It is surrounded by rich stands of mixed pine and hardwood forests, though back from the lake in all directions is rich farming country, typical of Southside Virginia. Travel to the lake takes anglers and other water lovers through acres of various agricultural crops. There is little development to threaten the lake. It is a quiet secluded lake that draws limited fishing pressure, partly because it lies between big Buggs Island Lake and the Leesville and Smith Mountain Lakes complex, all big water that is more attractive to many anglers.

This is a relatively shallow lake which favors anglers, the average depth being approximately 11 feet. Depths range from 2 to 3 feet along the shore and in the back of the coves to 13 to 14 feet behind the dam and in the flooded creek channel. There is much shallow water, 5 feet or less in the broad headwaters of the lake. A well-marked fish attractor is located across the lake from the boat ramp and is always worth checking out. Small weed beds are found in the shallows near the shore and in the headwaters. They provide good fish habitat and exciting top-water fishing.

Secondary Route 624 leads to the concrete boat ramp, and there is ample parking for automobiles and boat trailers back from the ramp. There is good bank fishing up and down the shore from the boat ramp, and a gated, little-used road provides good walking access from the parking lot.

The fish population is not as varied as it is in many other department lakes, but many anglers consider Lake Conner to be one of the best largemouth bass lakes in Virginia. In fact, it produced a state record back in 1985 that was checked in at 16 pounds, 4 ounces. Largemouth bass up to 14 or 15 inches are numerous. There are also strong populations of bluegills and redear sunfish up to 9 inches and a good population of channel catfish. This is chain pickerel country. The members of the pike family are native to this part of Virginia. They lived in the creeks flooded by the lake and still live in those streams draining into the lake. The department does not stock chain pick-

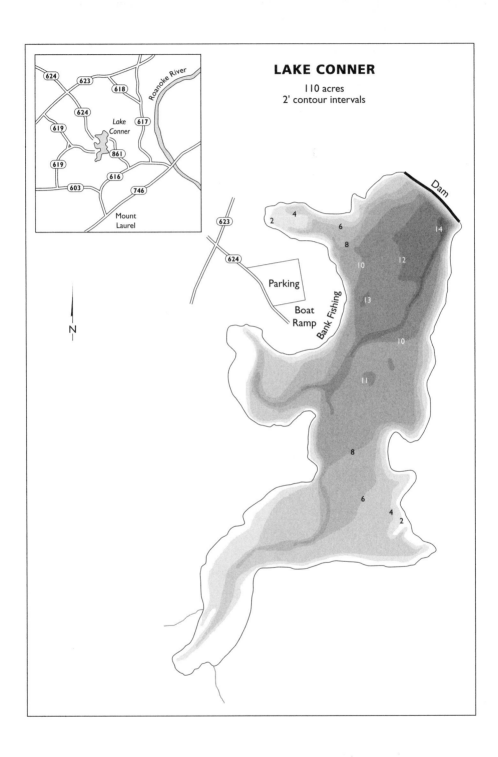

LAKE CONNER

110 acres
2' contour intervals

Roanoke River

624
623
618
624
619
Lake
Conner
617
619
861
746
616
603
623
624
Mount
Laurel

Parking

Boat
Ramp

Bank Fishing

Dam

N

2
4
6
8
14
10
12
13
10
11
8
6
4
2

erel and doesn't have to. They are vicious fish that strike dramatically and wage a good fight, often leaping and tail-walking across the surface.

No gasoline outboard motors are allowed on the lake, but an electric motor with a well-charged marine battery will get an angler to the choice fishing spots and back to the boat ramp with no difficulty. Sailboats and swimming are also prohibited, but canoes and johnboats are allowed. Bird-watchers and nature lovers can launch light canoes and quietly paddle the shoreline, alert for a great variety of wildlife native to Virginia. Whitetail deer are drawn to the water to drink, and waterbirds visit the shallows to feed on small fish. The lake is open to fishing 24 hours a day, and the fishing regulations are posted at the boat ramp or in the parking lot.

The boat ramp is located on one of the coves on the western side of the lake. An angler can launch his boat there, turn left and fish the deep water near the dam, or turn right and motor to the shallow water in the headwaters.

GAME REFUGE LAKE

SUPERVISING OFFICE: Department of Game and Inland Fisheries, Deep Creek, 3909 Airline Boulevard, Chesapeake, VA 23321. Telephone (757) 465-6811

LOCATION: Sussex County

SIZE: 30 acres

DIRECTIONS: Approximately 25 miles south of Petersburg or 15 miles north of Wakefield, take Secondary Route 602 east off Interstate 95. Travel east and cross Dobie Swamp, and turn right on a dirt road next to the first house on the right, a brick cottage with a chain fence around it. This road has no number or name but is used primarily for logging and hunting. Follow the road approximately one mile just beyond the power line crossing to the lake.

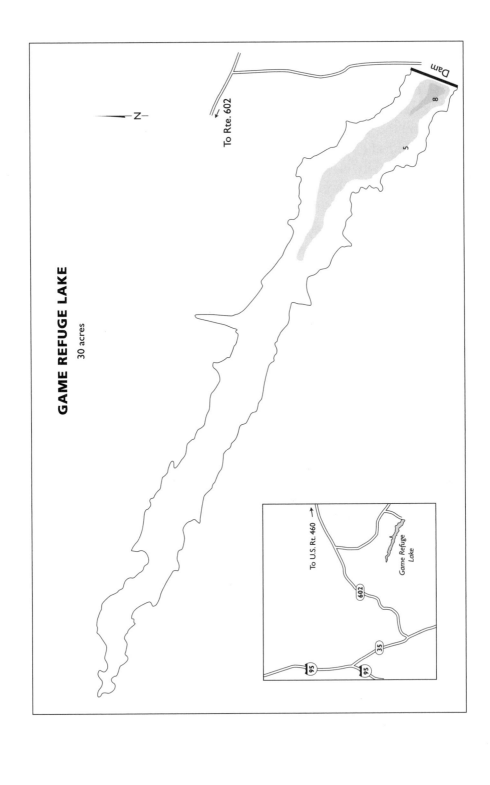

GAME REFUGE LAKE

30 acres

N

Dam

8

5

To Rte. 602

To U.S. Rt. 460

602

35

95

95

Game Refuge
Lake

This lake was built by the Civilian Conservation Corps (CCC) in 1935 and is located on the Virginia Department of Game and Inland Fisheries Sussex Tract property, 90 acres that are open to hunting, primarily for deer and ducks. The lake is an impoundment on Dick's Branch, a tributary of Dobie Swamp. The road off Route 602 is often muddy and rutted, and a four-wheel-drive vehicle is recommended. The aging dam built in 1935 is now breached, and very little of the lake remains. The department is removing it from its list of thirty-two managed fishing lakes, but the stream is still there, and a logjam against the dam has created some backwater. There are both chain and redfin pickerel in the stream, and the old road to the lake offers access to the stream for anyone interested in that kind of fishing. The lake held black crappie, bluegills, and largemouth bass, and there may be remnant populations in the stream or what remains of the lake. Anyone fishing it should realize, however, that the fishing will be tough.

LAKE GORDON

SUPERVISING OFFICE: Department of Game and Inland Fisheries, HC 6, Box 46, Farmville, VA 23901. Telephone (434) 392-9645

LOCATION: Mecklenburg County

SIZE: 157 acres

DIRECTIONS: Approximately 6 miles southwest of South Hill, take Secondary Route 664, Union Level Road, north and then right on Secondary Route 799 to the boat-launching ramp. From the north, take Route 664, Union Level Road, south from the hamlet of Union Level past Lake Gordon Road and then left on Route 799 to the boat-launching ramp. Secondary Route 664 crosses the outlet of the lake just below the dam, and the dam is visible from the road.

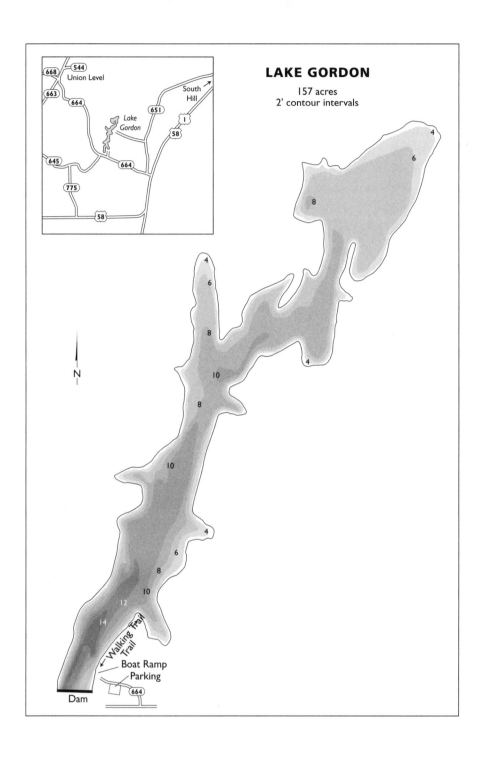

LAKE GORDON

157 acres
2' contour intervals

668 544
Union Level
663
664
651
Lake Gordon
1
58
645
664
775
58

N

4
6
8

4
6
8
10
8
4

10

8

4
6
8
10
12
14

Walking Trail
Trail
Boat Ramp
Parking
664
Dam

Impounded in 1949, Lake Gordon is one of the oldest department lakes in the state. Located in Mecklenburg County, it is one of the largest, too, though it is dwarfed by 50,000-acre Buggs Island Lake to the south, also in Mecklenburg County. The popular fishing lake is located in rolling farmland country and is in a very aesthetic setting. The lake is long and narrow with the narrowest part just behind the dam and the broadest at its headwaters. There is one deep cove on the north side of the lake beyond the midway point and a number of shallow coves that should receive the angler's attention. The lake area was not cleared of standing timber when it was impounded. As at Briery Creek Lake to the north, the dead timber and submerged stumps provide excellent cover for the fish. Fish find the logs, snags, and stumps good feeding areas, but they make it difficult to fish. There are probably enough lost lures in the lake to stock a modest-sized tackle shop. Most of this submerged wood is found in the upper reaches of the lake where the water is shallow. There are also patches of water lilies in the upper part of the lake, and they too provide excellent cover and good fishing. The lake is generally shallow, probably averaging 10 feet or less in depth. Water depths range from 4 feet or less in the headwaters and in the backs of coves to 12- to 14-foot depths near the dam and in the creek channel.

Lake Gordon is also one of the few department lakes where gasoline outboard motors are allowed, but they cannot exceed 10 horsepower. Anglers should be aware of the underwater obstructions that could damage an outboard motor. The concrete boat ramp is located near the dam, and there is a parking lot for automobiles and boat trailers in the same area. These limited facilities are located on the eastern side of the lake and a very short distance from Secondary Route 664.

There is good bank fishing near the boat ramp where a walking trail follows the shoreline. The dam, an easy walking distance from the parking area, is a favorite of bank fishermen, as evidenced by a well-worn trail that extends the length of the dam.

The fish population is rich. The largemouth bass fishing is good, with fish up to 7 pounds being fairly common. Good bass fishing can be found in the lily pads near the headwaters of the lake. This is shallow-water fishing, and surface lures can be productive. There is also good fishing for channel catfish, and chain pickerel, native to the waters of the area, offer some exciting fishing. Bluegills up to 7 inches long are the choice of many anglers, and black crappie and redear sunfish up to 8 or 9 inches also fin the water. Yellow perch, seldom found in other lakes in this area, are also present to give additional variety. The lake is lightly fished, possibly because big Buggs Island Lake is so nearby, but Lake Conner offers a different, more intimate kind of fishing that appeals to many serious anglers.

As is true of all department lakes, sailboats and swimming are prohibited. The fishing regulations are posted at the launching ramp and should be consulted before fishing. Nonanglers might enjoy launching a canoe and cruising the shoreline alert for birds and other wildlife, or they might like to go ashore in a quiet cove, locate a secluded spot, and enjoy a picnic. The agency owns 50 feet of the land back from the shoreline.

HORSEPEN LAKE

SUPERVISING OFFICE: Department of Game and Inland Fisheries, HC 6, Box 46, Farmville, VA 23901. Telephone (434) 392-9645

LOCATION: Buckingham County

SIZE: 18 acres

DIRECTIONS: From U.S. Highway 60 in the town of Buckingham, take Primary Route 638 to the Horsepen Wildlife Management Area sign on the left, follow the management area road to the bottom of a hill where the road forks. Take the right fork, and the dam is just a short distance up a steep hill. A very steep concrete boat-launching ramp is just up the lake from the dam. The dam is visible on the left as you drive up the hill to the parking lot.

This deep 18-acre lake is located within the 3,065-acre Horsepen Wildlife Management Area and is probably better known to hunters than to fishermen. The deer and turkey populations are strong. The area is heavily forested and hilly with many deep valleys. The lake is an impoundment on Horsepen Creek, a winding woodland stream for which both the lake and the wildlife management area are named. As is true of most of the Department of Game and Inland Fisheries lakes, sailing and swimming are prohibited, but unlike most of them, waterfowl hunting is permitted during the open waterfowl seasons, but on Wednesdays and Saturdays only. No other hunting is permitted, but trapping is allowed by permit. Gasoline outboard motors are prohibited, but electric-powered motors are permitted, as are canoeing and boating. The lake varies in depth from 2 feet or less at its headwaters to 20 feet at the dam. Much of the lower lake is in the 10- to 18-foot depth range.

The lake is located in a deep valley and is generally long and narrow with only shallow coves, although the boat ramp is located on a deep, narrow cove near the dam. The shoreline is generally wooded as the original stream flowed through a deep woodland valley with hardwoods predominant though there are some pines. Being remote and secluded, this small lake offers a unique opportunity for fishing in a quiet, peaceful atmosphere. There are numerous trails and roads throughout the area that will appeal to hikers. Primitive camping is permitted, as it is in all of the wildlife management areas.

Bank fishing is permitted, though much of the shoreline is all but inaccessible by foot. The road leading into the area and to the lake crosses Horsepen Creek below the dam and leads to a parking area on the opposite side of the lake from the boat-launching ramp. Some bank fishing should be available there.

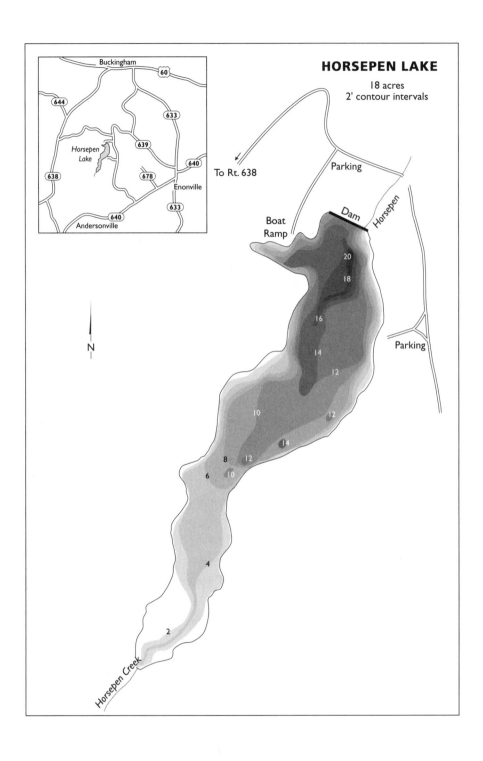

HORSEPEN LAKE

18 acres
2' contour intervals

Buckingham

60

644

633

639

640

Horsepen
Lake

638

678

Enonville

640

633

Andersonville

To Rt. 638

Parking

Boat
Ramp

Dam

Horsepen

20

18

16

14

12

Parking

N

10

12

14

8

12

6

10

4

2

Horsepen Creek

The concrete boat-launching ramp is adjacent to the vehicle parking area. It is short and very steep.

The fish population is rich, with largemouth bass, black crappie, bluegills, and channel catfish supporting much of the fishing. Over the years the bass have tended to run small, but they are plentiful. Bluegills run up to 7 inches in length and crappies a bit larger, some in the 8-inch range. This is also chain pickerel country, a popular fish native to Horsepen Creek. Some venture into the lake where they can grow to respectful size, but pickerel are not noted for prospering in impounded waters. Northern pike were once released in the lake but have not done well, but you never know when you might land a good one, a loner that has survived the releases years ago. The lake was drained in 2001 and then restocked. The department has also stepped up its management of the fishery. This bodes well for the future of the fishing in this small but picturesque lake.

LAKE NOTTOWAY (LEE LAKE)

SUPERVISING OFFICE: Department of Game and Inland Fisheries, HC 6, Box 46, Farmville, VA 23901. Telephone (434) 392-9645

LOCATION: Nottoway County

SIZE: 188 acres

DIRECTIONS: From U.S. 460 just west of Blackstone, take Secondary Route 606 north for approximately 5 miles. Route 606 will curve to the right and forks with Primary Route 607 but continue on 606, watching for a sign for the "Public Boat Landing." The turnoff to the lake is on the right less than a mile from the forks.

At 188 acres Lake Nottoway is one of the largest lakes in the system, and one of the few where gasoline outboard motors are allowed. They are limited to 10 horsepower or less, however. Fishing is allowed 24 hours a day. The lake was impounded

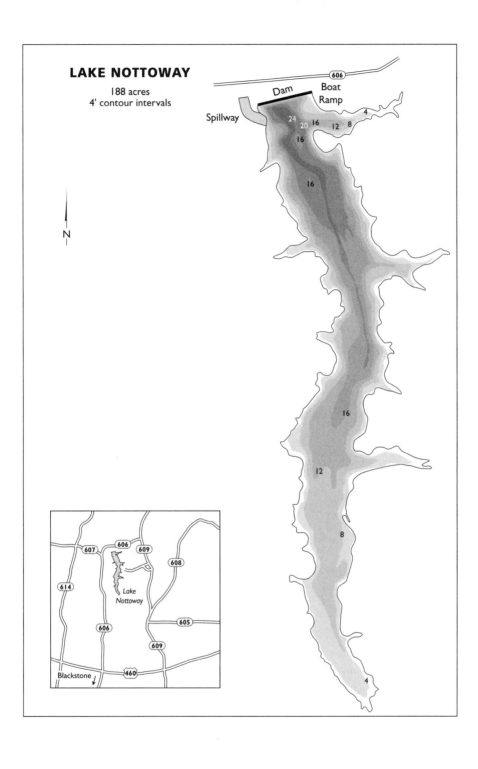

LAKE NOTTOWAY

188 acres
4' contour intervals

Dam

Boat Ramp

Spillway

606

24 20 16
16
8
4
12

16

16

16

12

8

4

N

606
607
609
608
614
Lake Nottoway
606
605
609
460
Blackstone

in 1978 and opened for fishing in 1980. It is located in farming country with good stands of mixed hickory, oak, and pine forests. The water is characterized by flooded standing timber, submerged piles of logs, and limited aquatic vegetation, all of which provide good habitat for a rich population of fish. Many local anglers refer to this as Lee Lake, but in Department of Game and Inland Fisheries literature it is Lake Nottoway.

The lake is long and narrow with numerous coves, many of them deep—particularly along the eastern shore. The water varies in depth from 4 feet or less at the lake's headwaters to 24 feet near the dam. From midlake to the dam, the water varies from 12 to 24 feet, with much of the water near the dam from 20 to 24 feet.

The concrete boat-launching ramp is located on a deep cove near the dam—across the dam from the spillway. There is ample parking space for automobiles and boat trailers near the ramp. There is also a courtesy pier for tying up a boat for loading.

The fish population in this large Southside Virginia lake is rich and varied. Largemouth bass up to 4 pounds are abundant, and the lake occasionally gives up some 10 pounders. Other popular fish include black crappie, bluegills, chain pickerel, channel catfish, and redear sunfish. The chain pickerel are native to the creeks and streams that feed the lake, but all the other fish have been introduced. Channel catfish are stocked every other year. Many of the various members of the sunfish family are in the ⅓- to ½-pound range.

While gasoline outboard motors of 10 horsepower or less and electric motors are permitted, sailboats are not. Nor is swimming allowed. The long shoreline of the lake hosts a great variety of songbirds and other wildlife. A canoeist paddling quietly along the shoreline should enjoy frequent sightings of wildlife.

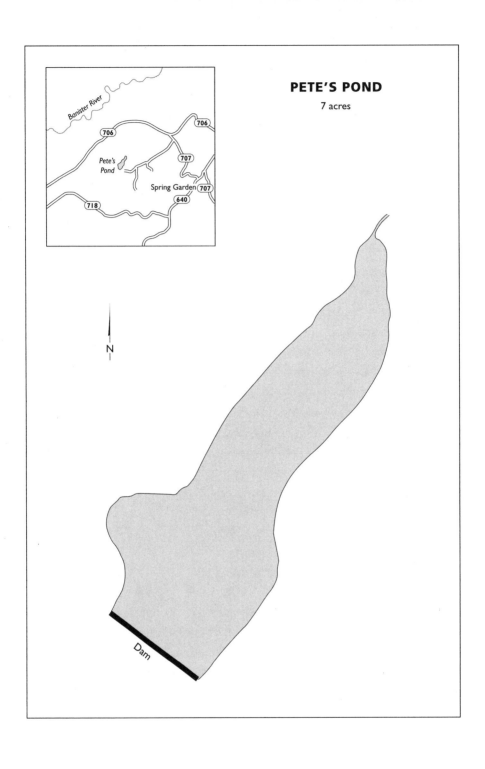

PETE'S POND

7 acres

Bannister River

706
706
707
Pete's
Pond
Spring Garden 707
718
640

N

Dam

PETE'S POND

SUPERVISING OFFICE: Department of Game and Inland Fisheries, 1132 Thomas Jefferson Road, Forest, VA 24551. Telephone (434) 525-7522

LOCATION: Pittsylvania County

SIZE: 7 acres

DIRECTIONS: From Chatham take Virginia Primary Route 57 east to Secondary Route 649 and look for the brown "Wildlife Management Area" sign on the right. Follow the entrance road to the pond. From U.S. Highway 29 south of Chatham, turn right on Secondary Route 640 and watch for brown signs indicating the route to the wildlife management area. The gravel road leading deep into the wildlife management area will fork at the maintenance headquarters. The one on the right leads to Pete's Pond, and the other, a short road, leads to the manager's residence—visible from the fork in the road.

Pete's Pond is located in the 2,712-acre White Oak Mountain Wildlife Management Area in central Pittsylvania County. At only 7 acres, it is the second smallest lake in the thirty-two-lake Department of Game and Inland Fisheries system of fishing lakes. The only smaller one is 3-acre Phelps Pond in the Phelps Wildlife Management Area in Fauquier County in the northern part of the state. Pete's Pond is the largest of several ponds located on the property, the others being once farm ponds that were on the property when the land was acquired for the wildlife management area. This is rolling farm country with elevations ranging from approximately 500 to 900 feet. Much of the area is covered with mixed hardwood and pine forests, but approximately a third of it is open land once cultivated for farm crops and now managed for quail, rabbits, and other small game as well as for deer and turkeys. It is popular among small-game hunters.

Access to Pete's Pond is good. A wildlife management gravel road ends at the pond where there is a launching area for cartop boats or canoes and ample parking space for automobiles and light boat trailers. Light trailered boats can also be launched, though the launching area is gravel only. Backing a trailer far into the lake is inadvisable. One of the other ponds, a small one, is located near the resident manager's dwelling. Fishing there is permitted from the bank only. Anglers should respect the manager's privacy and refrain from noisy activity. The other ponds are scattered about the property, and bank fishing only is allowed. Discarded Christmas trees have been placed along the banks to enhance the fishing. Check with the manager or other personnel regarding the location of the other ponds. Or better still, get a copy of the map of the wildlife management area from the Forest office of the Department of Game and Inland Fisheries. There are no roads leading to the ponds. They can, however, be reached by walking. Gasoline outboard motors are prohibited, but electric-powered motors are acceptable. Pete's Pond is so small that a couple of canoe paddles will suffice for most fishing. Sailboats and swimming are prohibited.

The fish population is rich and varied. Bluegills and redear sunfish, or shellcrackers, probably top the list, but the fishing for largemouth bass is good also. There is also a good population of channel catfish introduced by the department fisheries biologists. Grass carp have been stocked for the purpose of controlling the aquatic vegetation, which can take over a small body of water. These fish do not strike readily, but if one is caught, it must be released to the water unharmed. Fishing regulations are posted at the lakes or ponds.

Outdoor activities other than fishing abound here thanks to an excellent system of roads and trails. Maps of the wildlife management area can be obtained from the Department of Game and Inland Fisheries, or pick up a copy of *Enjoying Virginia Outdoors,* also published by the University of Virginia Press. It could prove handy for other lakes located on wildlife management areas. Hike the trails and enjoy the wildlife or camp on the property, but not near any of the ponds. Such camping is prohibited. Also take time to observe the extensive wildlife management practices being carried on continuously on the wildlife management area.

This is a small but unique body of water that can be a joy to fish and visit.

POWHATAN LAKES AND PONDS

SUPERVISING OFFICE: Department of Game and Inland Fisheries, 4010 West Broad Street, Richmond, VA 23230-1104. Telephone (804) 367-1000

LOCATION: Powhatan County

SIZE: 96 acres

DIRECTIONS: Take Secondary Route 684, Bell Road, north off U.S. Highway 60 just west of Powhatan to Secondary Route 625, Powhatan Lakes Road, then left on Route 625 to Powhatan Lakes. Where the road forks, take the left fork to the launching ramp on the upper lake and the right fork to the lower lake. A sign at the forks so indicates. For Powhatan Ponds, a short distance farther west on U.S. Highway 60, take Secondary Route 627 south and watch for the wildlife management area entrance on the left; follow the entrance road to Bass Pond where there is parking space and a gravel boat-launching ramp. There is also a gravel launching ramp on Sunfish Pond, but none on Bullhead Pond.

The Powhatan Lakes and Ponds, two lakes and three ponds, are located in the 4,462-acre Powhatan Wildlife Management Area that lies mostly south of U.S. Highway 60, which passes through Powhatan County.

The Powhatan Lakes, two of them, are long and narrow, the upper lake being a bit smaller of the two. They are adjacent to each other on a tributary of Sadler Creek. The upper lake was once an old millpond, and the foundations of the mill are vis-

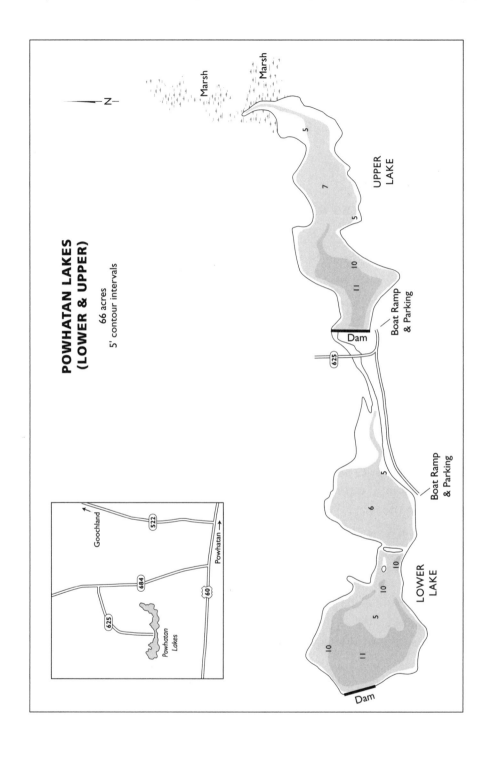

POWHATAN LAKES
(LOWER & UPPER)

66 acres
5' contour intervals

—N—

Marsh

Marsh

UPPER LAKE

5

7

5

10

11

Boat Ramp
& Parking

Dam

625

Boat Ramp
& Parking

5

6

10

10

LOWER LAKE

5

10

11

Dam

Goochland

522

684

625

Powhatan Lakes

60

Powhatan

ible just below the dam. The maximum depth near the dam is only 11 feet, and much of the lake is less than 6 feet deep. There is also a good deal of marshland at the headwaters. The concrete boat-launching ramp is adjacent to the parking lot near the dam. The parking area will accommodate several automobiles and boat trailers. The dam and a trail along the southern shoreline uplake from the parking area offer good bank fishing. The lower lake was apparently also the site of a mill. What appear to be islands in the narrow neck midway down the lake are the remains of the old dam. A new dam was built in the 1960s downstream from the remains, and it impounds the largest and deepest part of the lower lake, with most of the water being in the 10- to 11-foot range. Above the old dam the water averages only 5 to 6 feet. The lower lake road follows the southern shoreline, and on the upper reaches of the lower lake are a short concrete boat ramp and a parking area. The road also offers good bank fishing along the southern shore of the lower lake.

Together, the two lakes provide excellent bass fishing thanks to a good deal of shallow water and extensive patches of lily pads and other weeds. The fish populations are rich and varied, including largemouth bass, black crappie, bluegills, catfish, and redear sunfish. There should also be chain pickerel in both lakes as it is native to the streams in this part of Southside Virginia. The upper lake might provide the better bass fishing, with the lower lake offering a slight edge for crappies. These two lakes are secluded and surrounded by mixed pine and hardwood forests, an excellent setting for some quiet, undisturbed fishing. They are on a wildlife management area, of course, and during hunting seasons expect to see an occasional deer, squirrel, or turkey hunter back in the forests. Hunting and trapping are not allowed on the lakes, however, though trappers might be able to get permits. The lakes are open to fishing 24 hours a day.

POWHATAN PONDS

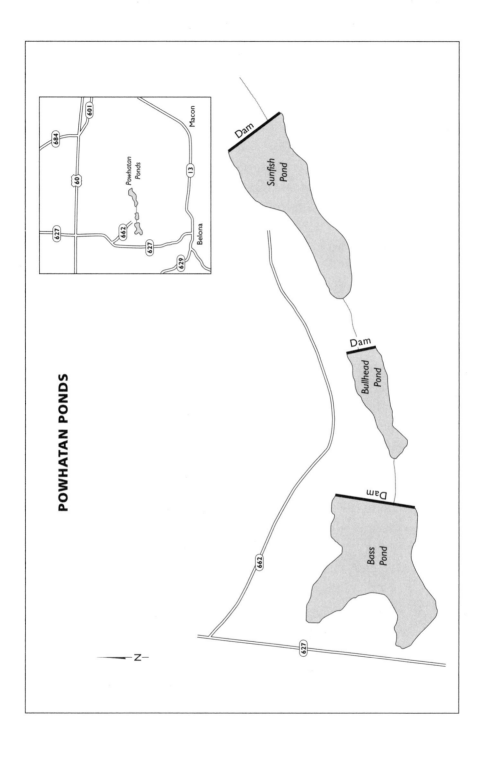

Gasoline outboard motors, swimming, and sailboats are prohibited, but electric motors are allowed, providing more than enough power to move freely about these two delightful little lakes.

Also located on the Powhatan Wildlife Management Area a short distance farther west off U.S. Highway 60 are the Powhatan Ponds, all impoundments on the same small stream. The upstream impoundment is called Bass Pond, and the downstream is known as Sunfish Pond. In between the two is the Bullhead Pond. Don't be misled by the names; the fish species are much the same in all three. They are nestled in the heart of the wildlife management area and are easily accessible. Secondary Route 662 off Route 627 leads to the parking lot near Bass Pond where there is a small graveled boat-launching ramp. Beyond Bullhead Pond, Route 662 continues downstream to Sunfish Pond where there is also a small graveled boat-launching ramp. There is none, however, at Bullhead Pond. The areas around the ponds have been cleared for bank fishing. Bass Pond is the upstream impoundment on the small feeder stream, followed by Bullhead Pond, with Sunfish Pond being the farthest downstream. While the gravel boat ramp provides boat access to Bass Pond, the open shoreline and the dam provide good bank fishing for those who do not own a boat or prefer to fish from the shore.

A rich and varied fish population includes largemouth bass, black crappie, bluegills, catfish, and redear sunfish. The two largest ponds, Bass and Sunfish, are considered to offer the best fishing, but giving Bullhead a try might offer some surprises.

Fishing hours and regulations are posted. They usually follow those for the wildlife management area. These unique little bodies of water receive light fishing pressure.

4 Southwest Virginia

THE COUNTIES OF Bland, Buchanan, Carroll, Craig, Dickenson,
Floyd, Giles, Grayson, Lee, Montgomery, Pulaski, Roanoke,
Russell, Scott, Smyth, Tazewell, Washington, Wise, and
Wythe

Southwest Virginia was Virginia's last frontier. While the early pioneers in this part of the state, the hardy explorers who ventured across rugged mountains, were defending their families against Indian raids and chinking their log cabins against the harsh Southwest Virginia winters, plantation owners along the tidal James River in the east were building spacious mansions and overseeing thousands of acres of fertile and flat farmlands. Southwest Virginia was a new world, a different world, a demanding world, even though the two diverse groups lived under the same colonial Virginia government. These extreme regions of Virginia, east and west, were vastly different—and still are.

Today Southwest Virginia lies generally from Roanoke west. Directly to the north the West Virginia line forms its border, and in the west it is bordered by Kentucky, all in mountain country. Directly to the south it is bordered by North Carolina and to the west by Tennessee. In the far southwestern tip of Virginia is Cumberland Gap through which Daniel Boone eventually located his long-sought route to Kentucky and its rich populations of game animals. He spent several years in Southwest Virginia hunting and exploring for that ideal route beyond the mountains. Today Lee and other far southwestern counties form what is loosely referred to as Deep Southwest Virginia. It's challenging and interesting country, and still a joy to visit.

Unlike the slow-flowing tidal rivers of the extreme eastern part of Virginia, the rivers here form in mountain country and race down into the valleys below. The New River is unique in Southwest Virginia in that it forms in the mountains of North Carolina to flow north through Virginia into the mountains of West Virginia, a river that flows north in a part of Virginia where most rivers flow south. Other major rivers such as the Clinch, Powell, and the three forks of the Holston flow south into Tennessee. The New is considered one of the oldest rivers in the world. In the far western part of the state near the Kentucky border, another river, the Pound, flows north to join the Russell River, which quickly leaves the state to head west into neighboring Kentucky.

Back in Daniel Boone's day the area offered good bear and deer hunting, both of which all but disappeared in the face of advancing civilization and unrestricted hunting. More recently, however, wise forest management on the part of the U.S. Forest Service and good wildlife management on the part of professional biologists of the modern Department of Game and Inland Fisheries have brought both back, and with them wild turkeys. The grouse hunting has always been good, as well as small-game hunting for rabbits and squirrels. Today there is also good duck hunting along the rivers and on the big reservoirs.

The big impoundments are more limited here than in other parts of Virginia, but Claytor Lake near Radford offers good big-water fishing, as does South Holston Lake. Much of that large lake, however, is in Tennessee. The dam is in Tennessee, and it is a Tennessee project. In the far west are Pound Lake and John W. Flannagan Reservoir, both impoundments on the Pound River and both popular fishing lakes.

Stream fishing is big in Southwest Virginia with its lofty mountains and green valleys through which flow fast streams. Several of the best trout streams in Virginia flow down the slopes of Whitetop Mountain and Mount Rogers, at 5,729 feet the highest mountain in Virginia. The region offers good fishing for native brook trout in wild streams and stocked trout in a number of designated trout streams. The smallmouth bass is equally popular with the New River, being possibly the best smallmouth bass river in Virginia. It vies with the James River in the east for that distinction. The South Fork of the Holston River is one of the top trout streams in the state. The popular smallmouth bass was introduced to these western waters where it prospered and now offers exciting fishing.

Largemouth bass in the lakes, smallmouth bass in most lakes and many streams, and native and stocked trout in singing mountain streams dominate the fishing in this unique region. The rock bass could well be the dominant panfish, but there are also bluegills, crappies, and redear sunfish. Channel and flathead catfish and walleyes round out the rich variety of angling possibilities.

In this interesting part of Virginia, there are only five Department of Game and Inland Fisheries lakes, but all are spectacular. Four are mountain lakes, and one is located in a fertile valley.

BARK CAMP LAKE

SUPERVISING OFFICE: Department of Game and Inland Fisheries, 1796 Highway Sixteen, Marion, VA 24354. Telephone (276) 783-4860

LOCATION: Scott County

SIZE: 48 acres

DIRECTIONS: At Tacoma on Alternate U.S. Highway 58, take Primary Route 706 South. Look for a brown sign on the highway. Approximately 4 miles south on Route 706 and just beyond the Jefferson National Forest sign, turn right on Primary Route 822. A brown "Bark Camp" sign indicates the proper road. Follow Route 822 approximately 2 miles to U.S. Forest Route 993 and follow that road to the lake and parking area.

The lake is located in the Clinch Ranger District of the Jefferson National Forest in an attractive recreation area that includes picnic tables, restrooms, and a modern campground with hookups. This is a joint project of the U.S. Forest Service, the U.S. Fish and Wildlife Service, and the Virginia Department of Game and Inland Fisheries, a very appealing area on a beautiful mountain lake surrounded by a mixed hardwood and pine forest in a rugged mountain setting. It is a beautiful spot to camp and loaf even if you do not fish, and it is easily accessible to thousands of people who live, work, and play in this far western part of Virginia. There is, of course, no swimming in the department lake. The lake is also referred to locally as Scott-Wise or Corder Bottom Lake.

The oldest Department of Game and Inland Fisheries lake in Southwest Virginia, it was completed in 1950 but was completely drained in 1978 to remove an unbalanced fish population. Once the lake returned to normal pool level, it was stocked with largemouth bass and bluegills. "It holds some big bass," said a fisheries biologist who monitors the fish population. Again in the early 1980s largemouth bass and additional northern pike fingerlings were stocked, this time in an effort to control the growing bullhead catfish and white sucker populations, fish that threatened to take over the lake. Since 1985 the lake has also been a put-and-take trout lake, meaning it is stocked periodically from October through May and twice monthly in March and April, top trout fishing months. From October 1 to June 15 it is designated trout water, meaning a trout fishing license is needed to fish for trout. A national forest stamp is required in addition to the regular state fishing license. From June 15 to October the trout license is not required,

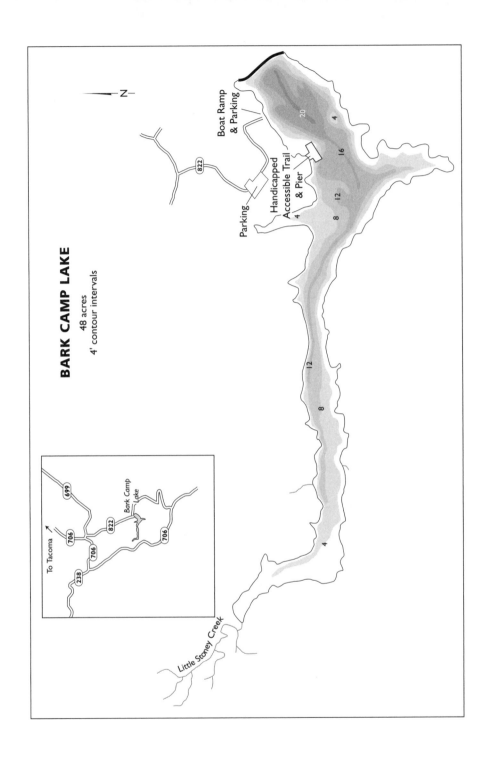

BARK CAMP LAKE

48 acres
4' contour intervals

–N–

Boat Ramp & Parking

Parking

Handicapped Accessible Trail & Pier

822

20

4

16

12

8

4

12

8

4

Little Stoney Creek

To Tacoma

699

706

822

706

706

238

Bark Camp Lake

although a state fishing license and a national forest stamp are still needed. Even though a trout fishing license is not required during this summer and early fall period, any trout caught may be creeled. And there are trout in the lake all year, not just during the stocking season.

The long, narrow lake is an impoundment in the Little Stony Creek valley. It has an average depth of only 4 feet, though there is some 20-foot water behind the dam. Much of the lake is in the 8- to 12-foot depth range. Little Stony Creek is a good trout stream in its own right, and it is stocked periodically from November through May. Many of these fish eventually end up in the lake.

The fishing facilities are excellent. There is a concrete boat-launching ramp with plenty of parking area near the dam and a courtesy pier for tying up a boat while it is being loaded or unloaded. Leading from the launching-ramp parking area down the lake to the fishing pier is an asphalt-paved trail for handicapped anglers. A wheelchair can be operated along this trail. There are also a pair of handicapped fishing piers. All of the facilities are located on the north side of the lake. Across the lake to the south, the shoreline is heavily forested. Much of the north side of the lake, however, is accessible for bank fishing.

As is generally true of department fishing lakes, swimming and the use of gasoline-powered outboard motors are prohibited. Canoeing, however, can be a delight, and electric motors are allowed.

The fish population is rich, including brown and rainbow trout, no doubt holdover fish from numerous releases of hatchery trout during the long stocking season. The mountain lake waters are cool throughout the year and hold trout well. Other species include largemouth bass, black crappie, bluegills, channel catfish, and possibly a few northern pike, remnant populations from the fingerlings stocked in the early 1980s. The cool waters favor this northern fish. The lake has produced several trophy-size largemouth bass. This northern strain of bass, accustomed to cold water, is a vigorous fish and fun to do battle with. The crappies are above-average size, and the bluegills and channel catfish are average size. An abundance of stumps and fallen trees provides good cover for fish, large and small. The shoreline fishing is good.

HIDDEN VALLEY LAKE

SUPERVISING OFFICE: Department of Game and Inland Fisheries, 1796 Highway Sixteen, Marion, VA 24354. Telephone (276) 783-4860

LOCATION: Washington County

SIZE: 61 acres

DIRECTIONS: On U.S. 19 approximately 7 miles south of Lebanon, look for a brown sign on the left indicating the route to the "Wildlife Management Area." Turn left into Virginia Primary Route 690, which leads to the Hidden Valley Wildlife Management Area. At top of a very steep grade, the road forks, and the left fork leads to the lake. From Abingdon take Alternate U.S. 58 and 19 and turn right at the sign into Route 690.

Virginia Primary Route 690, which leads to the lake, is very steep and best driven in a four-wheel-drive vehicle shifted into low gear. More than one angler has burned out a clutch in a truck or sedan pulling a heavy boat up that steep mountain road. Located in a deep valley in the Hidden Valley Wildlife Management Area, the 61-acre lake is long and narrow. It is an impoundment on Brumley Creek, which flows east through the wildlife management area. The road leading to the lake skirts the upper end of the lake, and anglers get a quick glance at the shallow flats in the upper end. The water here is less than 4 feet deep and filled with vegetation begging to be fished with top-water lures. This is a beautiful mountaintop lake that is surrounded by over 2 miles of forested shoreline. Like most of the lakes in Southwest Virginia, it is a high-elevation lake. The average depth is 14 feet, but there is a good stretch of 15- to 20-foot water behind the dam. Much of the upper reaches of the lake is shallow, as are narrow stretches of water near the shore all around the lake. Hidden Valley is a mountainous 6,400-acre wildlife management area purchased by the Department of Game and Inland Fisheries for public hunting. It is there for all outdoor lovers to enjoy, however, with plenty of room to roam, hike, hunt, camp, and just enjoy a rugged mountain environment. Brumley Mountain, the most prominent terrain feature, stretches about 4,000 feet.

The lake was constructed in 1964, and for the first fifteen years of its life, it was managed as a put-and-take trout fishery. In the 1980s, however, the lake was stocked with largemouth and smallmouth bass and redbreast sunfish to establish a warmwater fishery. It is no longer stocked with trout. The lake was drained in 1988 to repair the spillway and the emergency spillway. The lake was refilled, and in 1989 smallmouth bass, black crappie, channel catfish, and redbreast sunfish were introduced. From 1995 to 1997 walleyes were stocked to control an overabundance of sunfish, but they didn't produce a fishable population, nor did they control the sunfish. Largemouth bass also were introduced in 1997. They are expected to control the sunfish, and extensive weed beds and fallen trees provide ideal habitat for the popular fish. Largemouth bass taken from the cold mountain lake waters are vigorous and put up an exciting battle on light fishing tackle.

The fishing facilities are excellent. They are located on the north side of the lake off the road leading to the lake and ending at the dam. A concrete boat-launching ramp is near the midpoint of the lake with ample parking space for vehicles and boat trailers. Two additional parking lots are farther down the shoreline, one of which is near the dam. As is true of most department lakes, swimming and the use of gasoline-powered outboard motors are prohibited. Electric outboard motors,

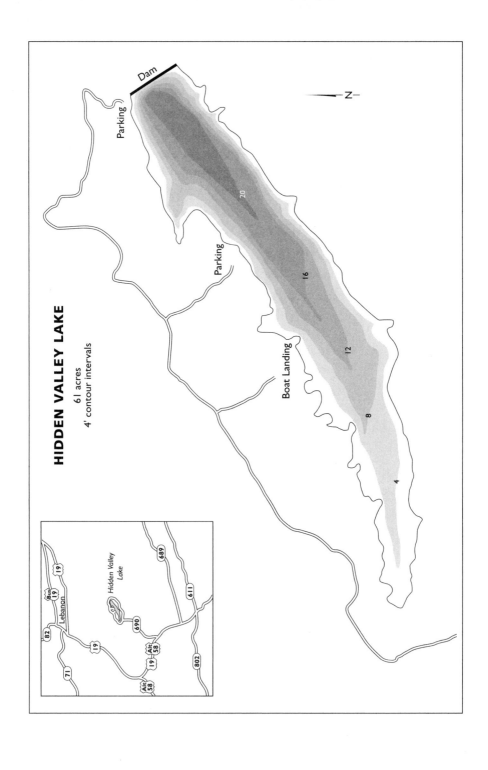

HIDDEN VALLEY LAKE

61 acres
4' contour intervals

Dam

Parking

Parking

Boat Landing

20

16

12

8

4

—N—

Hidden Valley Lake

Lebanon

82

71

Bus 19

19

19

19

Alt 58

Alt 58

690

689

611

802

however, are permitted. Bank fishing is possible around most of the lake, but the dam and several cleared areas along the shore facilitate this relaxing kind of fishing.

Located in the Hidden Valley Wildlife Management Area, the setting is true wilderness with no signs of civilization. Primitive camping is permitted in the wildlife management area, and there are numerous hiking trails. The Jefferson National Forest stretches away to the east. Fishing regulations are posted at the boat-launching ramp, but the lake is open to fishing all year. The surface is often covered with ice during extreme winter weather.

KEOKEE LAKE

SUPERVISING OFFICE: Department of Game and Inland Fisheries, 1796 Highway Sixteen, Marion, VA 24354. Telephone (276) 783-4860

LOCATION: Lee County

SIZE: 92 acres

DIRECTIONS: The hamlet of Keokee near the Kentucky border in Lee County is within a few minutes of Keokee Lake. To reach the lake take Alternate U.S. Highway 59 and 23 north from Big Stone Gap, turn west on Virginia Primary Route 68, which becomes Secondary Route 606 on top of the mountain at the Lee County line. Mountain ridges are often used to mark county boundaries. Turn south or left off Route 606 onto Virginia Primary Route 623 and then Route 622, which leads to the lake.

"Keokee" is a tongue twister. Place the emphasis on "okee" when pronouncing it. Pronounce it incorrectly, and some local citizen will set you straight in a hurry. At 92 acres Keokee Lake is the second largest of the five Southwest Virginia Department of Game and Inland Fisheries lakes. Only Laurel Bed Lake at 300 acres is larger. It is located in the Clinch Ranger District of the Jefferson National Forest and just a "stone's throw" from

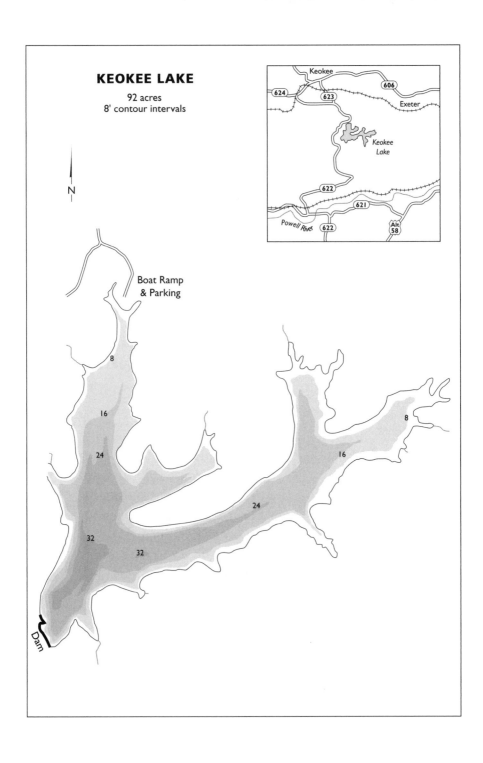

KEOKEE LAKE

92 acres
8' contour intervals

N

Boat Ramp
& Parking

8

16

24

32

32

Dam

8

16

24

Keokee

624

623

606

Exeter

Keokee
Lake

622

621

Powell River

622

Alt
58

the Kentucky border. It was impounded in 1975, flooding a heavily wooded mountain valley. The timber was left standing in an effort to provide ideal habitat for the fish, but most of the trees have since rotted at the water's surface and broken off, leaving stubs standing. This has created a hazard for boat traffic. The standing timber also failed to provide the fish habitat hoped for, and as a consequence the lake was drained early in 2001, and much of the fallen timber was removed. That done, the lake was then refilled. The lake was originally stocked with a Florida strain of largemouth bass, but the southern fish could not adapt to the cold Southwest Virginia mountain water. They were then replaced by a northern strain of largemouth bass, a vigorous fighting fish. But even the hardier strain of bass did not do well. "The mountain streams feeding into the lake were highly infertile," said a department fisheries biologist, "so we fertilized the lake well before refilling it." Aquatic vegetation flourishes in the shallow areas of the lake and offers good habitat for bass and panfish. The lake is surrounded by approximately 4 miles of forested shoreline. The average depth of the water is 17 feet, but there is some very deep 32-foot water behind the dam. Depths in the lower reaches of the lake range from 24 to 32 feet.

The lake is basically two long prongs, one running almost due north from the dam and the other northeast. Several smaller arms also probe deeply into the heavily forested shoreline. The shallow water is pretty much limited to a narrow strip along the shore and back reaches of the several arms. Even there the water drops off quickly to 8 feet or more.

The facilities are first-class, including a concrete boat ramp, a paved parking area, and restrooms, all convenient to the boat ramp. The boat ramp and the other facilities are located at the end of the road near the back of the prong running north from the dam. From the boat ramp you look south toward the dam. An angler access trail has been cleared all around the lake, but bank fishing is limited because access to the heavily forested shoreline is difficult. Future plans call for an accessible fishing trail that will allow anglers to fish from the bank all around the lake.

Fish populations include the largemouth bass, mostly of the northern strain, but remnant populations of the Florida strain may still remain. Other fish include bluegills, channel catfish, and redear sunfish. Over the years the lake has turned up some excellent catches of bass in the 10- to 12-inch range and an occasional trophy. The sunfish, however, offer the best fishing, with some large bluegills and redear sunfish. The best fishing for the big sunfish occurs during the summer months.

Only electric-powered outboard motors are allowed on the lake, and swimming is prohibited. Probing the various arms of the lake in a slowly paddled canoe, alert for birds and other forms of wildlife, could be productive. Two hiking trails begin near the boat ramp on the northern arm of the lake. One called the Keokee Loop Trail runs for almost 4 miles, and the other is the 2½-mile Olinger Gap Trail. Both are in the Jefferson National Forest.

LAUREL BED LAKE

SUPERVISING OFFICE: Department of Game and Inland Fisheries, 1796 Highway Sixteen, Marion, VA 24354. Telephone (276) 783-4860

LOCATION: Russell County

SIZE: 300 acres

DIRECTIONS: Take Virginia Primary Highway 80 south off U.S. Highway 19 east of Lebanon to Virginia Secondary Route 613 and left on 613 to Virginia Primary Route 747 and along Big Tumbling Creek into Clinch Mountain Wildlife Management Area and follow the signs to the lake. From the south take Virginia Primary Highway 107 north to Saltville, and from Saltville take Virginia Secondary Route 634 to Allison Gap, then left on

Route 613 to Route 747, turn right and follow Route 747 into the wildlife management area, and then follow the signs to the lake.

Laurel Bed Lake is located on top of Clinch Mountain in the Clinch Mountain Wildlife Management Area at an elevation of 3,600 feet. The wildlife management area at 25,477 acres is one of the largest in Virginia, and while it was purchased and is managed for hunting, it offers a great variety of outdoor recreation opportunities. The lake impounds Laurel Bed Creek, which flows into Big Tumbling Creek, a popular fee-fishing trout stream operated by the Department of Game and Inland Fisheries. Laurel Bed Lake was constructed in 1967 to augment the flow in Big Tumbling Creek. A sustained flow of cold water is needed to support the trout fishery. The lake serves that purpose, but it also has produced some excellent fishing for native brook trout over the years. It was managed as a native brook trout fishery during the 1970s and 1980s, but during the early 1990s a combination of acidic water and strong competition from a flourishing rock bass population reduced the growth rate of the brook trout, and the fishing faded. The lake was drained in 1996 for repairs, and fisheries biologists took advantage of the water drawdown to remove the rock bass. Also to improve the water quality of the lake and make it less acidic, a helicopter was employed to lime the lake, delivering approximately 50 tons of limestone to the upper stretches of the lake and to its feeder stream, Laurel Bed Creek. This provided positive results, and the lake was restocked with brook trout. Smallmouth bass were added with the hope that they would keep the rock bass population under control. This seems to be working, as the lake furnishes good fishing for both brook trout and smallmouth bass. The rock bass are still there, but their numbers are under control. But they too furnish good fishing. There is an abundance of natural food in the lake, and native brook trout are expected to thrive on this food supply. Fingerling brook trout were stocked in 1997.

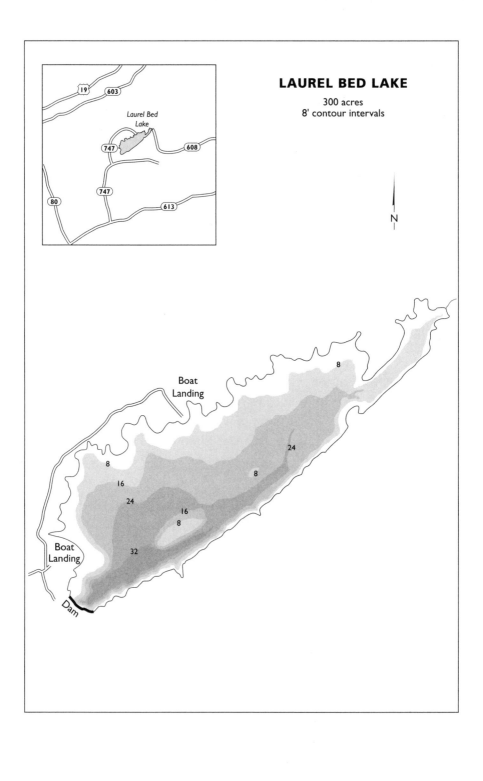

LAUREL BED LAKE

300 acres
8' contour intervals

N

19 603

Laurel Bed
Lake

747 608

80 747

613

Boat
Landing

8

24

8

8

16

24

16

8

Boat
Landing

32

Dam

This fairly large lake could well be the most spectacular body of water in the thirty-two-lake department system. It is surrounded by a second-growth forest of hemlock and mixed hardwoods with a good mix of aspen and cherry trees. It gives the impression of a northern lake with hemlock, spruce, and other trees and vegetation more abundant to the north. The heavily forested 6-mile shoreline that surrounds the lake slopes gently and is easily accessible for bank fishing. There are a few weed beds in the shallow part of the lake, but fallen trees and stumps of trees provide most of the habitat.

The average depth of the lake is 15 feet, but deeper water up to 32 feet is found behind the dam. The deep water along the southern shore ranges from 24 to 32 feet. The northern shore waters from the dam to the lake's headwaters average 8 feet or less. The deep water back of the dam offers good fishing during the hot summer months.

Fishing facilities are excellent. The entrance road winds along the northern shore, and there are two boat-launching ramps off this road. The downlake ramp is make of concrete and located near the dam. The upper boat-launching ramp is located midway the length of the lake and is made of gravel, but it offers good access to the lake, particularly for small boats. There is ample parking space for automobiles and boat trailers at both boat ramps. Primitive camping is provided throughout the wildlife management area, and the Virginia Department of Conservation provides a developed campground in the wildlife management area approximately 4 miles from the lake. There are no amenities such as hookups and running water, but there are designated campsites, fireplaces, and picnic tables. Swimming and gasoline outboard motors are prohibited, but electric motors are legal. This is a beautiful lake on which to launch a canoe and paddle quietly along the shoreline alert for songbirds and other forms of wildlife. There are also miles of hiking opportunities in the wildlife management area and nearby Jefferson National Forest.

Fishing for bass and trout is the primary outdoor activity here, but there are almost unlimited opportunities for others who enjoy Virginia's outdoors. Just downstream from the dam is Big Tumbling Creek, a popular fee-fishing trout stream that is stocked regularly with legal-size trout.

RURAL RETREAT LAKE

SUPERVISING OFFICE: Department of Game and Inland Fisheries, 2206 South Main Street, Suite C, Blacksburg, VA 24060. Telephone (540) 961-8304

LOCATION: Wythe County

SIZE: 90 acres

DIRECTIONS: From Interstate 81 take exit 81 south on Virginia Secondary Route 749, turn right on Route 677, and then left on Route 778, and proceed to the lake concession stand and the boat ramp. Follow the brown signs that designate the route to Rural Retreat Lake and Recreation Area.

Unlike most of the department lakes in Southwest Virginia, Rural Retreat is located in a beautiful limestone valley surrounded by fertile farming country. The fertile soils and water rich in nutrients contribute to a healthy and thriving fish population. The lake is long and narrow, but two arms to the west form a peninsula on which the boat ramp and concession stand are located. The concession stand is open during the warm months of the year. There is an abundance of shallow water, though depths range up to 35 feet behind the dam. At 90 acres it is a relatively large lake as department lakes go. Its shoreline is surrounded by open grasslands for the most part, and the bank-fishing opportunities are abundant, though most anglers launch their boats at the easily accessible ramp near the concession stand. Weed cover near the shoreline provides near ideal cover attracting insects and small fish that in turn attract feeding bass and other fish that fin the lake's fertile waters. Except for the pair of deep coves in the upper end of the lake, most coves are small and shallow, leaving a reasonably straight shoreline. The shoreline generally pitches gently into the water, though there are a few steep banks. One is near the campground across the lake from the concession stand. While the amount of shallow water is much more abundant than in most lakes, particularly the mountain lakes in Southwest Virginia, there is also a good deal of deep water, particularly back from the dam. The water there drops off to 30 to 35 feet. There is also a good bit of water in the 20-foot depth range in the creek channel well up the lake, but it is a narrow strip. Much of the lake is in the 5- to 10-foot range. The fishing could be good in the deep water during the hot summer months when fish leave the shallows during the hotter parts of the day.

Facilities on this spectacular Southwest Virginia lake are excellent, making it attractive not just to anglers but for all who turn to the outdoors for pleasure and relaxation. The easily accessible boat ramp has two roomy parking areas, a luxury not available at most department lakes where parking is available but often limited. Many of the facilities are linked to the concession stand, which offers limited fishing tackle and snacks. There are also rental boats available at the concession stand, and while swimming is not allowed, as is typical of department lakes, access to a nearby swimming pool and bathhouse is available at the concession. There is also a developed campground directly across the lake from the concession stand, reached by Secondary Route 778, which continues beyond the concession and bridges one of the two uplake prongs of the lake. There are also picnic facilities available for those who simply want to enjoy a picnic and loaf for a few hours in a delightful setting.

Typical of department lakes, in addition to swimming, gasoline outboard motors and hunting are prohibited, though electric motors are allowed.

The fish population in this fertile valley lake is rich and abundant. Largemouth bass, black crappie, bluegills, and chan-

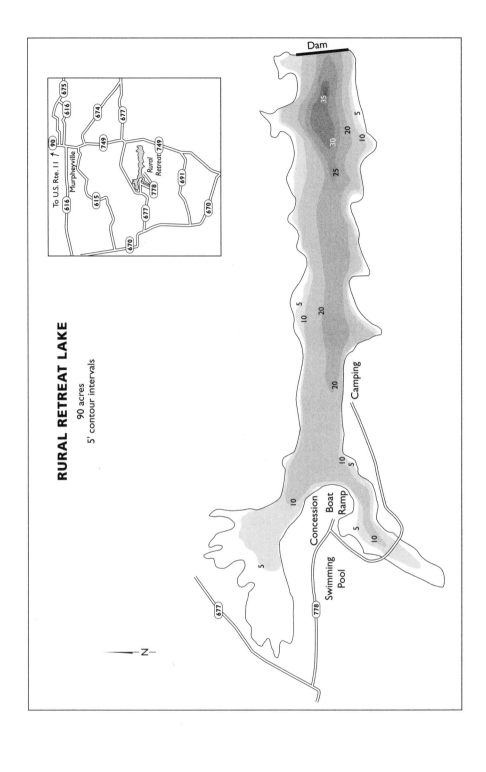

RURAL RETREAT LAKE

90 acres
5' contour intervals

Dam

Camping

Concession
Boat
Ramp

Swimming
Pool

-N-

To U.S. Rte. 11
Murpheyville
Rural
Retreat

nel catfish support most of the fishing, but muskie and northern pike also have been introduced. Fishing for muskie is slow regardless of where you find them, but boating a big one can be an exciting and rare angling experience, and that experience awaits the angler who has the time and patience to fish for this elusive fish. Fishing for muskie calls for large lures or big minnows, too large for most fish, but even a hungry bluegill will attack a bait or lure that is almost as big as it is. In the course of fishing for muskie, an angler is almost sure to get the attention of other smaller fish. That includes northern pike that were introduced to the lake more recently than their close kin, the muskie. The fishing regulations are posted at the boat ramp and should be consulted before going on the water. They are changed from time to time as the condition of the fish populations demands.

To appreciate the diversity of fishing in Southwest Virginia, take a look at Rural Retreat Lake in the rich farming valley and then drive northwest up the mountains to Laurel Bed Lake, just a short distance away. The two lakes are a good example of the diversity of fishing opportunities the angler can enjoy in Southwest Virginia.

5   Upper Piedmont and Coastal Plain

THE COUNTIES OF Albemarle, Arlington, Amherst, Caroline,
Charles City, Culpeper, Essex, Fairfax, Fauquier, Fluvanna,
Greene, Goochland, Hanover, Henrico, James City, King and
Queen, King William, Loudoun, Louisa, Madison, Middlesex,
Nelson, New Kent, Orange, Prince William, Rappahannock,
Spotsylvania, and Stafford

This chapter deals with a part of the state not so clearly defined as the Northern Neck, Southside Virginia, or Southwest Virginia. The lakes here are in the most densely populated part of Virginia, including the big metropolitan areas of Richmond and Northern Virginia, the suburban sprawl of the nation's capital, Washington, D.C. Smaller population centers such as Charlottesville and Fredericksburg are also slowly gobbling up open spaces. Big open fields where hunters once went after quail and rabbits are now filled with modern houses and big backyards where the cries and laughter of children at play now replace the mating call of the bobwhite quail and the excited squeals of little beagle hounds hot on the trail of a fleeing bunny. But despite the high demands made on its waters, the fishing remains good, thanks in no small part to good fisheries management. Providing good fishing in such a densely populated region is a real challenge for the Department of Game and Inland Fisheries, but the agency seems to be handling it.

Busy Interstate 95 runs north and south through this region, carrying a load of constant traffic, easily one of the busiest highways in America. To the west, U.S. Highways 15 and 29 run north and south through the central part of the region. To the south Interstate 64 runs west out of Richmond to connect with Interstate 81, and to the north Interstate 66 carries Washington D.C., area traffic west to join Interstate 81. Populations are also building rapidly along these major highways.

This interesting part of Virginia lies north of the James River, south of the Maryland-Virginia border, and west of the Potomac River to the crest of the Blue Ridge Mountains. It's mostly rolling hill country, though there are acres of flatlands along the lower reaches of the major rivers, modified coastal plains. To the west the region claims some of the highest peaks in the majestic Blue Ridge Mountains range.

Despite this growing sprawl of suburbia, we find a lot of good fishing water in this region. The Department of Game and Inland Fisheries owns and manages nine fishing lakes that are scattered throughout the area. An angler doesn't have to travel far to find good fishing water close to his or her home, spectacular water that it is a joy just to be on. In addition to the department lakes, there are other impoundments such as 10,000-acre Lake Anna, a rich and productive lake that receives heavy fishing pressure but still provides good fishing year after year. There are also a number of smaller ones such as 670-acre Lunga Reservoir on the Marine Corps Reservation at Quantico, 800-acre Lake Manassas, and 2,100-acre Occoquan Lake. All of these lakes are treated in the next chapter.

Major rivers in this region offer good stream fishing. The broad Potomac River forms the boundary between Maryland and Virginia. It is actually owned by Maryland, but an agreement between the two states allows licensed Virginia anglers to fish its productive waters. It is tidal from Washington, D.C., to its confluence with the Chesapeake Bay. To the south the big James River forms the general boundary between Southside Virginia and the upper piedmont, the region under consideration here. In between are the Rapidan and Rappahannock Rivers. The Rappahannock is also tidal from Fredericksburg downstream to its confluence with the Chesapeake Bay. The Rapidan forms as a famous trout stream along the eastern slopes of the Blue Ridge Mountains and flows into the Rappahannock upstream from Fredericksburg. Other fast trout streams racing down the eastern slopes of the Blue Ridge Mountains offer fishing for both native brookies and hatchery-reared trout. The upper reaches of the James, Potomac, Rapidan, and Rappahannock Rivers offer good smallmouth bass fishing, as do a number of their smaller tributaries.

Freshwater fishing in this unique part of Virginia offers opportunities for a great variety of fish, including both largemouth and smallmouth bass, bluegills, catfish, chain pickerel, crappie, rock bass, and even a few muskie, northern pike, and walleye, the last three being exotic fish introduced by the Department of Game and Inland Fisheries.

In this increasingly densely populated part of Virginia, it would appear that there are limited hunting opportunities, but some of the most ardent hunters in America live and hunt here. Drive the back roads in the region, and you will pass through large well-managed grain and cattle farms where big flocks of geese feed and extensive stands of hardwood timber where squirrels and turkeys find ideal habitat. It is mostly private land, of course, but permission to hunt much of it can often be obtained. It is also a region of strong deer populations, which cause problems in counties like crowded Fairfax County where hunting is limited. The Potomac River offers good duck hunting, and jump shooting for ducks is popular on many of the other streams including the James River. The sprawling military reservations, including the Quantico Marine Corps Base and Fort A. P. Hill, offer thousands of acres of public hunting land. There is also the Rapidan Wildlife Management Area in Madison County where black bear hunting is popular. This big public hunting area along the eastern slopes of the Blue Ridge Mountains also offers good hunting for deer, grouse, squirrels, and turkeys.

Crowded? Sure, but the fishing and hunting are there for those willing to work for it.

In this interesting and challenging part of Virginia, there are nine well-managed Department of Game and Inland Fisheries lakes, many of which have excellent fishing facilities, some of the best fishing facilities in Virginia on some of the best-managed fishing waters. The fishing pressure on these lakes demands good fisheries management, and the biologists of the Department of Game and Inland Fisheries work hard to provide it.

LAKE ALBEMARLE

SUPERVISING OFFICE: Department of Game and Inland Fisheries, 4010 West Broad Street, Richmond, VA 23230-1104. Telephone (804) 367-1000

LOCATION: Albemarle County

SIZE: 35 acres

DIRECTIONS: From U.S. Highway 29 or the U.S. Highway 250 Bypass at Charlottesville, take Barracks Road west. It eventually becomes Garth Road and Secondary Route 614. Continue on this road to Lake Albemarle Road, Secondary Route 675, and turn left at the brown "Public Fishing Lake" sign. Follow Route 675 to the lake. At the dead end take the right fork, on Route 669, and the boat-launching ramp is a short distance from the fork.

Lake Albemarle is the oldest of the department's thirty-two fishing lakes. It was built by the Civilian Conservation Corps, the old CCC, in 1938 to provide, in addition to fishing, other water recreational opportunities, primarily swimming. This was the depth of the Great Depression, and recreational opportunities were rare in western Albemarle County. It became a popular spot with a swimming beach and a large concession building. It drew crowds from all over Albemarle County and adjoining counties as well as Charlottesville and other nearby communities. In 1979 the swimming beach and concession

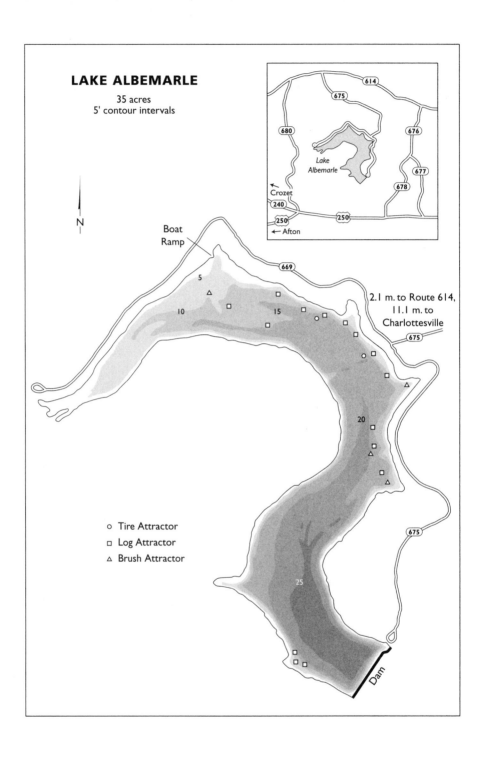

LAKE ALBEMARLE

35 acres
5' contour intervals

N

Boat
Ramp

669

2.1 m. to Route 614,
11.1 m. to
Charlottesville

675

5

10

15

20

25

○ Tire Attractor
□ Log Attractor
△ Brush Attractor

675

675

Dam

614
675
680
676
677
678
Lake
Albemarle
Crozet
240
250
250
Afton
250

were closed, and the lake was turned over to the Department of Game and Inland Fisheries for public fishing. Fishing and limited boating are about the only uses at present. There is no hunting, and gasoline-powered outboard motors are prohibited. Electric motors are permitted and popular. Sailing and paddleboats are prohibited.

The lake is formed by a dam in a small, winding stream valley, and it takes the shape of a horseshoe as it winds north, west, and then south in the heavily wooded valley. The boat ramp is on the north side just as it bends south, a short distance from Route 675. The boat ramp is unpaved but short and easy to access. It lies in a little valley near what was once a popular swimming beach. A small courtesy dock is nearby, providing facilities for tying up a boat while loading or unloading. There is also ample parking space for automobiles and boat trailers. The road beyond the boat ramp is unpaved but extends along the western shore of the lake to its headwaters. This is mountain foothills country, and the lake is long and narrow. The water is deep behind the dam, 25 feet or more, and water in the 15- to 20-foot depths extends up the lake almost to the boat ramp. There is some deep water of approximately 35 feet at the outlet tower near the dam. The water at the boat ramp is in the 5- to 10-foot range, and a narrow strip of water of 5 feet or less near the shore pretty much rings the lake, with a more extensive stretch of shallow water near the headwaters.

A good deal of fish habitat improvement work has been done in the lake, some of it by local anglers or angling clubs. Most of it is on the north side of the lake extending from the boat ramp down the lake to the dam. On the south side of the lake near the dam is a trio of log attractors. The remains of an old diving tower left over from the days when the lake was popular for swimming forms an excellent fish habitat near the boat ramp. Most of the attractors, about fifteen of them, are located in approximately 10 feet of water. Downed trees near the shoreline, which were cut by anglers or beavers or felled during storms, also offer good habitat. Many of these are along the southern shore across the lake from the manmade attractors. A more or less permanent population of beavers has added its own unique kind of habitat, brush piles that in the past have held good populations of crappie during the spring months. The crappie fishing, unfortunately, has seemed to decline. Now the attractors appeal mostly to the abundant population of largemouth bass. The shoreline is heavily wooded by mixed pine and hardwood forests, and a few hillside residences are set back from the lake. Bank fishing is popular, and the roads, Route 675, which ends at the dam, and Route 669, which leads from the fork past the boat ramp to the headwaters of the lake, offer many opportunities to fish from the shore. The far side of the lake from the boat ramp is generally inaccessible.

At only 35 acres, this hill country lake is not large, but it offers a good variety of fish, including largemouth bass, bluegills, and redear sunfish, more popularly known as shellcrackers. There is also a good population of pumpkinseed sunfish, usually small but colorful. The largemouth bass population is strong, but the lake is not noted for trophy bass.

Aside from its attraction as a fishing lake, now its primary role, the lake offers an opportunity to launch a canoe and work the long shoreline alert for a variety of wildlife. A flock of Canada geese usually inhabits the lake as well as some colorful little wood ducks. Beavers work the lake constantly. A canoeist, paddling slowly and quietly, might get amazingly close to these interesting critters, but suddenly one will spot the canoeist, slap the water with its broad tail, and disappear beneath the sparkling surface of the lake.

The boat ramp is located near the former swimming beach, a popular recreation area before and after World War II, a time when recreation opportunities were rare for many rural people. It filled a need, but possibly the lake's major contribution to the outdoor world is that it kicked off the thirty-two-lake public lakes fishing program of the Department of Game and Inland Fisheries that now embraces most of Virginia.

LAKE BRITTLE

SUPERVISING OFFICE: Department of Game and Inland Fisheries, 1320 Belman Road, Fredericksburg, VA 22401. Telephone (540) 899-4169

LOCATION: Fauquier County

SIZE: 77 acres

DIRECTIONS: From U.S. Highway 29 north of Warrenton and near New Baltimore, take Virginia Secondary Route 600 east to Secondary Route 793, turn right and proceed to Route 825, which leads to the lake. Look for brown signs for "Public Fishing Lake Brittle" at Route 600 on U.S. 29 and at Route 793 off Route 600.

Lake Brittle, opened for fishing in 1955, is one of the oldest of the thirty-two Department of Game and Inland Fisheries fishing lakes. In a densely populated region, it is just 30 miles from the Washington, D.C., Beltway 495, which circles the nation's capital. It was constructed with Dingell-Johnson funds, generated by an excise tax on fishing tackle raised at the federal level and distributed to the states on the basis of the number of fishing licenses sold annually. The entrance road leads to the boat ramp, a courtesy pier for tying up boats while being loaded and unloaded, a concession stand, and a fishing pier, all located near the dam. From the boat ramp you can see only the lower end of the lake, for most of the upper stretches are blocked from view by a broad wooded peninsula that extends deeply into the lake from the southern side. It forms a narrow neck in the lake, but up the lake from this peninsula, the lake spreads out, offering a broad expanse of reasonably shallow water running from 2 feet or less near the headwaters of the lake to 10 to 15 feet near the peninsula. Mixed pine and hardwood forests surround much of the lake, giving it a peaceful setting in a part of the state where the pace of life is fast and there is the constant sound of busy highway traffic and air traffic overhead. The always busy Reagan Airport is nearby, and there is the con-

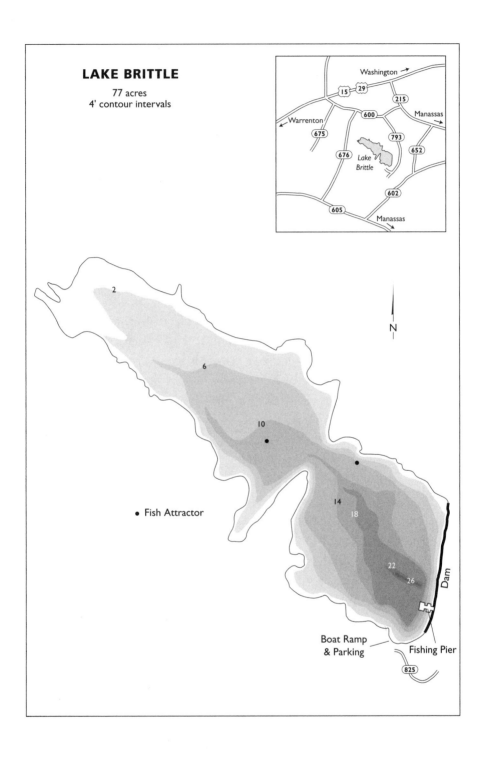

LAKE BRITTLE

77 acres
4' contour intervals

Washington
15 29
215
600 Manassas
Warrenton
675 793
676 652
Lake
Brittle
602
605
Manassas

2

6

10

N

14

• Fish Attractor

18

22

26

Dam

Boat Ramp
& Parking

Fishing Pier

825

stant noise of planes taking off or preparing to land. The tranquillity and peace of the lake and its surrounding forests offer a pleasant contrast to the busy world where it is located.

The lake averages approximately 7 feet in depth but has a depth of approximately 25 feet near the spillway tower. Several fish attractors have been placed in the lake, one below the narrow arm of the lake and the other just above it. These are marked by buoys, and the wise angler will give them some attention.

The lake is jointly owned and operated by the Virginia Department of Game and Inland Fisheries and the Fauquier County Parks and Recreation Department. There are a number of residences around the lake, but they are well back from the shoreline. While the lake is open to fishing all year, the concession is usually open from March 15 into October.

In addition to the boat ramp and courtesy pier, there is a fishing pier accessible from the dam on the lower end of the lake. The concession, when open, offers rental boats and electric outboard motors for use on the rental boats or on private boats launched at the ramp. Fully charged batteries are also available for rental. Also available are a variety of baits, limited fishing tackle, and snacks. Gasoline outboard motors, hunting, sailing, and swimming are prohibited.

While fishing is the major attraction, there is a good bit of wildlife that uses the lake much of the year. Ducks are often seen on the water. This is top resident Canada goose country, and usually there is a big flock on the water. Just watching them coming in, dropping their feet, and landing can offer hours of relaxation. Brittle is a popular lake for those few who enjoy ice fishing, and ice fishermen enjoy the added pleasure of watching the geese. When the lake is mostly covered with ice, there is often a stretch of open water near the point of the peninsula. The geese are apparently aware of this open water, and late in the day they flock to it to roost, usually arriving in small groups. It is an interesting spectacle worth driving to the lake late on a cold winter day and just watching this work of nature. As is true of most department lakes, hunting is prohibited, though trapping permits might be available upon request.

Despite its other attractions, Lake Brittle is first a fishing lake, and a good one. The water holds a good population of largemouth bass, with fish averaging 2 to 3 pounds, though fish up to 6 pounds are fairly common. There is a slot limit in effect which says all largemouth bass of 12 to 15 inches in length must be returned unharmed to the water, but this could be changed. Check the fishing regulations that are posted near the boat ramp closely before embarking on a fishing trip. There is also a good redear sunfish population where the average fish is approximately a half pound. Channel catfish are stocked annually, and the average cat weighs 2 pounds, an ideal size for table use. Walleye are stocked to maintain a predator population, and anglers take some big ones. Bluegills and crappie round out the fish population. Lake Brittle has long been home to an abundant gizzard shad population which serves as forage fish for the bass and other species. The little fish can quickly overpopulate the lake, however, and to control them the department biologists introduced flathead catfish back in 1990. Anglers catching a flathead, however, are asked to release it so it can continue with the control of the highly prolific gizzard shad.

In addition to fishing, the lake offers picnic tables and restrooms in the vicinity of the concession stand, and many non-fishermen like to go there just to enjoy a picnic, do a little hiking, enjoy nature, and simply relax in a quiet and picturesque setting.

BURKE LAKE

SUPERVISING OFFICE: Department of Game and Inland Fisheries, 1320 Belman Road, Fredericksburg, VA 22401. Telephone (540) 899-4169

LOCATION: Fairfax County

SIZE: 218 acres

DIRECTIONS: Burke Lake is located north of Virginia Primary Route 123 between Interstate 95 to the south and Interstate 66 to the north. From Interstate 95 turn right on the entrance to Burke Lake Park, and from Interstate 66 turn left. A brown sign indicates "Burke Lake." Route 123 is also known as Ox Road. Follow signs to the marina and boat ramp. There is also a Department of Game and Inland Fisheries boat ramp down the lake near the dam. A paved road within Burke Lake Park leads to the department ramp.

At 218 acres Burke Lake is the largest Department of Game and Inland Fisheries lake in the region and one of the largest in the state. It is also probably the most heavily fished and most intensively managed by the department. It has to be so managed to maintain good fishing in the face of such pressure. Someone has expressed the opinion that it is the most heavily fished lake in America, a statement that might or might not be true. Being located within the ever-lengthening shadows of Washington, D.C., the nation's capital, it does suffer heavy fishing pressure. Because of this pressure it is heavily fertilized by department fisheries managers. The fertilizer creates green-tinted water that might bother some anglers. It does not harm the fish but instead produces more natural food and a healthy fish population. Burke Lake is the main attraction in Burke Lake Park, one of the largest parks in Northern Virginia. The park is managed by the Fairfax County Park Authority and offers a great variety of recreational opportunities. The lake, however, is owned and managed by the Department of Game and Inland Fisheries. It has a number of well-marked fish attractors and 5 ½ miles of shoreline for anglers who like to work a shoreline or fish from the shore. A unique feature is Vesper Island, almost directly across the lake from the marina and near the northern shoreline. Fishing the island shoreline can also be productive.

There is some deep water in the stream channel behind the dam, ranging from 25 to 35 feet at the dam. Much of the water in the upper stretches is in the 10- to 15-foot range. Up the lake

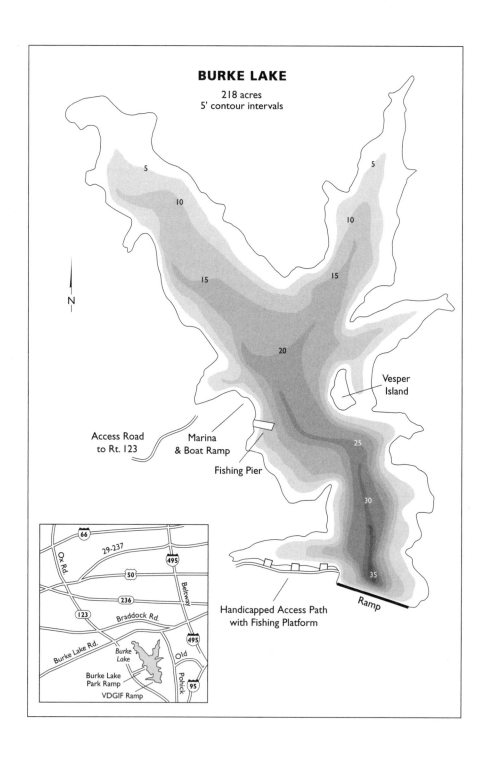

BURKE LAKE

218 acres
5' contour intervals

N

5

10

15

5

10

15

20

Vesper
Island

25

30

35

Access Road
to Rt. 123

Marina
& Boat Ramp

Fishing Pier

Ramp

Handicapped Access Path
with Fishing Platform

66
Ox Rd.
29-237
495
50
Beltway
236
123
Braddock Rd.
Burke Lake Rd.
Burke
Lake
Old
Pohick
95
Burke Lake
Park Ramp
495
VDGIF Ramp

from Vesper Island there are two deep prongs, one running almost due north and the other westward toward the headwaters of the lake. Much of the water in the backs of these prongs is 5 feet or less in depth and offers some good shallow-water fishing. There is a smaller prong almost directly across the lake from the marina and several more shallow ones down the lake. While fishing is the big attraction for anglers, there is a great variety of other outdoor recreational opportunities within the big park. Swimming, sailboats, and gasoline-powered outboard motors, however, are prohibited, as is typical of department lakes. Fishing and other regulations regarding the use of the park and its facilities are posted at the marina. Electric-powered outboard motors are permitted. Normally the lake is open to fishing only while the park is open, but again it is best to check the regulations posted at the marina. There are two boat-launching ramps, the one at the marina and a Department of Game and Inland Fisheries ramp down the lake near the dam. There is a handicapped-accessible fishing pier on a prong of the lake near the dam which is lighted at night. The light on the water attracts insects that in turn attract small baitfish. The night crappie fishing from the pier is good because the fish are attracted to the lighted area by the small fish feeding on the insects. There are also restrooms at the marina and picnic areas with tables. A shoreline biking and hiking trail provides an opportunity to stretch your legs plus access to good bank fishing. There are also campgrounds for anglers who want to mix family camping with fishing. Finally there are facilities for golfers including driving ranges and 18-hole golf course. Jogging is popular, with a number of trails available. Many of these trails also offer opportunities to enjoy wildlife, or you can launch a canoe and paddle slowly and quietly along the long shoreline, keeping your eyes open for birds and other wildlife.

Fishing opportunities are excellent and varied. The major species include largemouth bass, bluegills, channel catfish, black crappies, and redear sunfish, or shellcrackers. The bluegills and redear sunfish average about a quarter of a pound, and the crappie are a bit heavier, all good panfish and delicious on the table. The largemouth bass population is one of the best in all of the department lakes, mostly a result of intensive management including fertilizing. Fish over 6 pounds are fairly common, and the average is in the 3-pound range. The bass are subjected to heavy fishing pressure, however, and are not easy to catch, a real challenge for even expert anglers. The abundant forage-fish population also keeps them well fed and less inclined to take the angler's offering. The lake may be best known among anglers, however, for its muskie fishing. They are the lake's trophy fish, with many tipping the scales at 20 to 25 pounds. The big fish are stocked periodically to provide diversity for anglers. Good muskie fishing is a rarity in Virginia. Burke Lake also provides brood fish for the department's muskie-rearing program. The fish are netted during the spring spawning season and stripped of eggs, which are shipped to department hatcheries where the fish are reared to fingerling size and stocked in other suitable waters throughout the state. Walleyes, an excellent table fish, are also stocked periodically and grow to trophy size in the well-fertilized water. The fish average 3 pounds in weight, but many grow to trophy size. Some healthy 9- to 10-pound walleyes lurk in the deep water and occasionally end up in some lucky angler's creel. Obviously the angling opportunities in this Northern Virginia lake are varied and interesting.

LAKE CURTIS

SUPERVISING OFFICE: Department of Game and Inland Fisheries, 1320 Belman Road, Fredericksburg, VA 22401. Telephone (540) 899-4169

LOCATION: Stafford County

SIZE: 90 acres

On U.S. 17 north of Fredericksburg, or exit 133 west off Interstate 95, turn right on Secondary Route 616, Poplar Road, then left off Route 616 onto Secondary Route 662, which leads to the lake. Driving south on U.S. Highway 17, the turn into Route 616 is to the left. To visit Curtis Memorial Park, continue on Route 662 to Secondary Route 612 and turn left. Watch for brown signs to lake or park.

This picturesque fishing lake, owned and managed by the Department of Game and Inland Fisheries, lies near the boundary of Curtis Memorial Park, which is owned and operated by the Stafford County Parks and Recreation Department. The lake, however, was constructed with fishing as its primary goal. Though not in the shadows of Washington, D.C., as are Lake Brittle and Burke Lake to the north, it does serve a densely populated part of Virginia, including nearby Fredericksburg and the sprawling U.S. Marine Corps Base at Quantico a few miles to the north. Fishing is popular among Marines. Large stands of timber were left standing when the lake was formed to provide habitat for a healthy fish population, including some lunker largemouth bass. A lot of this timber is on the right up the lake from the boat-launching ramp on the north side of the lake. In addition to hardwood trees, the rising water covered dense thickets of cedar, ideal cover for a variety of fish and also a good place for anglers to hang up and lose some lures, a small price to pay for the thrill of doing battle with a 10- to 12-pound bass. The lake occasionally gives up 12- and 13-pound largemouth bass. While providing ideal habitat for bass and other fish, this standing timber can also create risks for the angler. Rotting limbs occasionally fall into the water, and trees rot and break off at the waterline. Anglers are advised to stay out of the timber during storms or high winds. Under such conditions it is best to stay off from the timber and cast to it, staying beyond the range of the tallest timbers. Eventually all of these trees will rot and break off at the waterline, leaving stumps or stubs that will remain for years after the trees above the water rot and fall.

LAKE CURTIS
90 acres
4' contour intervals
612
662
616
Potomac Run
Lake Curtis
Boat Ramp
Washington, D.C.
754
616
Warrenton
17
Hartwood
Rappahannock River
1
95
Fredericksburg
N
4
8
12
Access Road to Rt. 662
16
Fishing Pier
Boat Ramp
4
12
16
12
8
20
24
Dam

They will then a present a hazard for boats, though boats propelled by electric motors do not move fast enough to sustain substantial damage. Curtis is a beautiful lake surrounded for the most part by hardwood forests, though a golf course borders part of it.

While the water behind the dam approaches depths of 30 feet, the average depth is only 9 feet. Much of the upper lake ranges from 4 feet or less to 8 to 10 feet, good fishing water. The southern shore of the lake, directly across from the boat-launching ramp, is characterized by several prongs and a number of shallow coves, inviting the attention of anglers. The lake is generally long and narrow, with the upper stretches beyond the midway point bending toward the south.

Facilities at the lake are few but adequate. The concrete boat-launching ramp is shallow and easy to access from a roomy parking lot for automobiles and trailers. Other facilities include a handicapped-accessible fishing pier and a courtesy pier— both at the boat ramp and parking lot. There is also a Porta-Potty restroom nearby. The lake is open to fishing 24 hours a day.

As is typical of department fishing lakes, swimming, gasoline-powered outboard motors, and sailing are prohibited. Otherwise small boats such as canoes and johnboats are permitted for fishing, of course, but also for nature watching or just the joy of paddling a canoe along an interesting shoreline. Electric-powered outboard motors are permitted and popular. Nearby Curtis Park offers a swimming pool, tennis courts, and picnic facilities. Rental boats are available from the Stafford Parks and Recreation Department at the park.

Lake Curtis is an excellent fishing lake, thanks in no small part to the abundance of habitat left in the water when the lake was formed. Leaving standing timber in the lake has worked wonders in some lakes such as Briery Creek and Curtis but has been seemingly less effective in high mountain lakes such as Keokee. Lunker largemouth bass that fin the waters of

Lake Curtis could well be its top angling attraction. The water consistently gives up lunker-size bass and has been known to produce some 13-pound lunkers. Some of the largest bass in Northern Virginia are caught in Lake Curtis. The bluegill fishing is also good. For many anglers the bluegill is a favorite fish despite the presence of the more glamorous largemouth bass. The fishing for channel catfish is also good, and the department fisheries stock fingerling catfish periodically. Bluegills generally can hold their own without additional releases once they are established. They are very prolific little game fish. The standing timber appeals to crappie here just as it does in Briery Creek Lake. Fishing the standing timber for crappie can be challenging as well as productive. The species of crappie introduced here is the black crappie, generally considered our native crappie. It is the crappie introduced to most department lakes. The white crappie, found in some of the larger reservoirs, such as Buggs Island Lake, is slightly larger, but it is not native to Virginia. Many anglers do not recognize the difference between the two popular fish, but the black crappie is slightly smaller.

FLUVANNA RURITAN LAKE

SUPERVISING OFFICE: Department of Game and Inland Fisheries, 4010 West Broad Street, Richmond, VA 23230-1104. Telephone (804) 367-1000

LOCATION: Fluvanna County

SIZE: 50 acres

DIRECTIONS: From the community of Cunningham on Virginia Primary Route 53, turn west on Secondary Route 619 and follow the signs to the lake. Look for the brown sign at the intersection of Routes 53 and 619, and watch for the sign on the right where the gravel road from Route 619 leads to the lake. From the west take Virginia Secondary Route 620 north off Virginia Primary Route 6 at Kidds Store and follow it to Route

619 and then proceed east on Route 619 and turn left into the lake. Kidds Store is approximately 6 miles east of Scottsville.

The road leading from Route 619 to the lake becomes steep and curved as the lake is approached. There are actually three levels near the lake. The upper level, which is approached first, is the parking area for vehicles and boat trailers. The second or middle level is a turnaround area where the vehicle and boat trailer can be positioned for backing the boat down the concrete ramp and launching it in the lake. The third or bottom level is the lake itself at the bottom of the ramp. There is also a courtesy pier near the ramp where boats can be tied for loading and unloading. It is not a fishing pier. Even though the lake is located in gently rolling piedmont country, the boat ramp is probably the steepest and most difficult to maneuver of those at all the lakes in the system. An angler should by all means use a four-wheel-drive vehicle when pulling his boat out of the lake and up the long, steep launching ramp. Fluvanna Ruritan Lake was an early 1950s project of the Fluvanna Ruritan Club. Working closely with the Department of Game and Inland Fisheries, members located the land and arranged for its transfer to the department, hence its name. Locally it is simply called Ruritan Lake. It was constructed in 1956, and the department assumed management of it as a public fishing lake. The remnants of an old mill that was once located on the banks of the stream impounded to form the lake remain in the lake in approximately 10 feet of water. This fish attraction is located near the center of the long, narrow lake. A steep and heavily forested cliff forms the southern shoreline of the lake. The mature hardwood forest provides a touch of autumn as the water cools in the fall, and in the spring mountain laurel adds color to that same shoreline. Directly across the lake from the launching ramp, the northern shore is also mostly forested, but a few homes have lawns that run to the water's edge. The launching ramp is a short distance up the lake from the dam, and directly to the left of the ramp facing up the lake there is a long, deep cove that gets a lot of

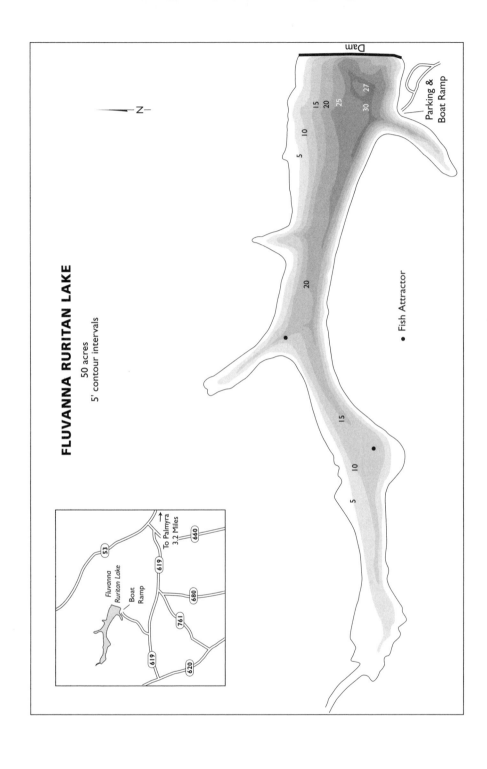

FLUVANNA RURITAN LAKE

50 acres
5' contour intervals

—N—

Dam

Parking &
Boat Ramp

Fish Attractor

5
10
15
20
25
30
27

20

15

10

5

Fluvanna
Ruritan Lake

Boat
Ramp

53

619

To Palmyra
3.2 Miles

619

680

761

620

660

attention from anglers. There is also a deep cove midway up the northern shore of the lake. There is a fish attractor in the mouth of that cove and another across the lake at the mouth of a much shallower cove. The water near the dam ranges from 25 to 30 feet in depth, but the depth drops off to 15 to 20 feet midway up the lake. There is good deal of shallow water of 5 feet or less near the headwaters. Anglers should be aware of tree stumps in the shallow water, left when much of the lake was cleared before its impoundment. They present a hazard for boats, particularly when the water level is low. These shallows are popular in late spring among fly-rod anglers who like to fish small popping bugs for bedding bluegills. Bluegill fishing can also be good just behind the dam later in the summer. The fish like to move into the narrow patch of vegetation bordering the dam to feed and then retreat quickly to deep water behind the dam should danger appear. In addition to its excellent blue-gill fishing, the lake is also noted for its crappie fishing. Many successful crappie fishermen simply troll up and down the lake, especially during the spring months. Later in the season fishing the stump-filled water in the headwaters can produce crappie. There is also a good population of largemouth bass, though the fish do not run large. A good population of redear sunfish adds to the rich variety of angling possibilities. Northern pike, tiger muskellunge, and walleyes also have been introduced, but none has produced a viable fishery, and the stocking of these exotic fish has been discontinued. A few anglers successfully fish for channel catfish, though they are not stocked frequently. The lake is heavily fertilized once a year, and fisheries manag-ers say this doubles the poundage of fish that would live there under normal conditions. Bank fishing is popular along the dam and in the area between the launching ramp and the dam. The deep cove to the left of the launching ramp is also popular among shore fishermen. As is generally true of the department lakes, gasoline outboard motors and swimming are prohibited. Electric motors, however, are allowed and popular among anglers. The Ruritan club has placed several picnic tables near the parking lot, and they are available for public use. The lake was drawn down in 2002 and renovated before being reopened to fishing.

LAKE NELSON

SUPERVISING OFFICE: Department of Game and Inland Fisheries, 1132 Thomas Jefferson Drive, Forest, VA 24551. Telephone (434) 525-7522

LOCATION: Nelson County

SIZE: 40 acres

DIRECTIONS: Lake Nelson is located east off U.S. Highway 29 between Charlottesville and Lynchburg. Follow Secondary Route 655, Arrington Road, east to the hamlet of Arrington and then left on Secondary Route 812, Lake Nelson Lane, to the lake. "Turn at the ice cream sign" is the usual advice you get if you ask for directions in the Lovingston area. The ice cream shop is located across Route 29 from the entrance road.

Located in the heart of Nelson just south of Lovingston, the lake gives the angler a magnificent view of the Blue Ridge Mountains to the west. The lake was impounded in the middle 1950s and opened to fishing in 1958. Later, in 1966, the lake was drained, renovated, and reopened to fishing again in 1969. It now offers good fishing for a rich variety of fish.

The concrete boat ramp and a courtesy dock are located a short distance up the lake from the dam and are reached by Route 812, which runs along the southern shore of the lake. The courtesy dock or pier is for the convenience of anglers for loading their boats after launching or for unloading before leaving the lake. The concrete boat ramp is convenient to Route 812 and offers a quick and easy access to the lake. There is a roomy parking area for automobiles and boat trailers.

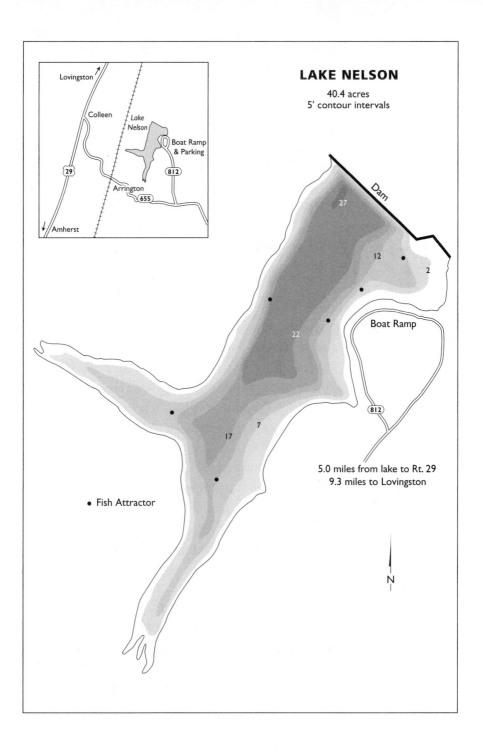

LAKE NELSON

40.4 acres
5' contour intervals

Lovingston

Colleen

Lake Nelson

Boat Ramp & Parking

29

Arrington

655

812

Amherst

Dam

27

12

2

Boat Ramp

22

7

17

812

5.0 miles from lake to Rt. 29
9.3 miles to Lovingston

• Fish Attractor

N

There is also good bank fishing on the shoreline reached from Route 812. In fact, there are even benches along the shore for relaxing or keeping an eye on a fishing bobber. A concession stand nearby is open during the warmer months of the year, but there are no rental boats available. There is also a public campground in the vicinity of the concession stand, but it is privately operated. Secondary Route 812 circles the campground and leads back toward Arrington.

Typically of the department lakes, electric outboard motors only are allowed. Gasoline outboard motors, sailboats, and swimming are prohibited. This is an anglers' lake built with their fishing license money and reserved for fishing. Fishing regulations including size and creel limits are posted near the boat ramp and should be consulted before fishing the lake.

From a maximum depth of 32 feet behind the dam, the depths drop off to 5 feet and less near the shore and in the headwaters. In addition to the headwaters of the main feeder stream, a long prong of the lake extends northwest across the lake from the area of the boat ramp. There are at least a half dozen fish attractors scattered about the lake. One is located in the mouth of the deep cove across the lake from the boat ramp. All are well marked and worth checking out when fishing the lake.

The variety of fish in Lake Nelson is rich, offering an equally rich variety of fishing opportunities. The species include largemouth bass, bluegills, blue and channel catfish, and redear sunfish, more popularly known as shellcrackers. The growth rate of the largemouth bass is greater than that found in most Virginia waters. And unlike most department lakes, there are both black and white crappie. Blue and channel catfish in the 20-pound range often end up in Lake Nelson anglers' creels. Grass carp have been introduced to control the vegetation and are off-limits to anglers. There is an outside chance at the best that an angler would catch one, but any caught should be returned to the water immediately. The carp feed on vegetation and are rarely interested in the angler's offerings.

LAKE ORANGE

SUPERVISING OFFICE: Department of Game and Inland Fisheries, 1320 Belman Road, Fredericksburg, VA 22401. Telephone (540) 899-4169

LOCATION: Orange County

SIZE: 124 acres

DIRECTIONS: A short distance north of Orange on Virginia Primary Route 20, the Constitution Route, a brown "Public Fishing Lake" sign marks the intersection of Route 20 and Virginia Secondary Route 629. Go south on Route 629 to Secondary Route 739, Lake Orange Road. Turn left and drive to the lake. From the east, Route 629 off U.S. Highway 522 leads to the turnoff to the lake. From this direction, turn right to the lake.

An impoundment on Clear Creek, Lake Orange at 124 acres is one of the largest of the department lakes. With an average depth of 14 feet, it is also one of the deepest. The depths range from 36 feet or more behind the dam to 4 feet or less in the headwaters of the lake, in the back of some of the coves, and along much of the shoreline.

This picturesque lake, constructed in 1964, is located in rolling farming country in the piedmont region of the state, and well-managed farmlands form much of its shoreline. The southern shoreline is mostly hardwood forests, however, and mixed pine and hardwood forests also form some of its northern shoreline, particularly that in the lower end toward the dam. An unusual feature of the lake is a long narrow prong that runs a northerly direction from the dam. A casual look down the lake from the boat-launching ramp will not reveal this unique part of the lake, and it is often overlooked—and probably the lightest fished area of the big lake.

Lake Orange Road, the access to the lake from Route 629, leads onto a long, narrow peninsula near the center of the lake. The boat ramp, concession stand, and other facilities are located on this peninsula. It is also a popular spot for bank fish-

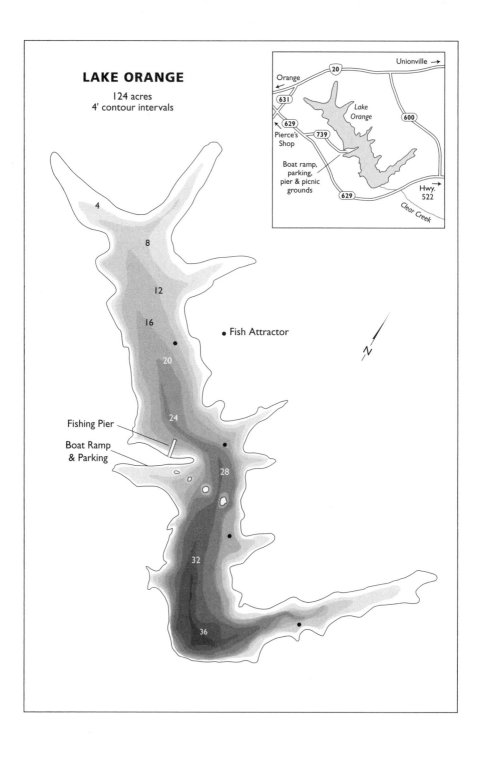

LAKE ORANGE

124 acres
4' contour intervals

4

8

12

16

20

• Fish Attractor

24

Fishing Pier

Boat Ramp
& Parking

28

32

36

N

Unionville →

Orange

20

631

Orange

Lake
Orange

629

600

Pierce's
Shop

739

Boat ramp,
parking,
pier & picnic
grounds

629

Hwy.
522

Clear Creek

ing, with a tiny island just offshore. An easily accessed concrete boat ramp is located here as well as a courtesy pier where boats can be tied for loading and unloading. There is also ample parking space for automobiles and boat trailers. A concession stand offering live bait, limited fishing tackle, and snacks is open from March through October. There are also restrooms, a picnic shelter, picnic tables, and grills. And across the peninsula from the launching ramp is an excellent handicapped-accessible fishing pier. The crappie fishing is good there during the spring season. The concession rents boats complete with electric motors, batteries, and life jackets during the warmer months of the year. Otherwise the lake is open all year, and private boats can be launched at the ramp. Gasoline outboard motors, sailboats, and swimming are prohibited. Like all of the department lakes, Lake Orange is for anglers only.

The lake is fertilized regularly by the Department of Game and Inland Fisheries managers and is rich in nutrients, assuring a healthy fish population. A quartet of fishing attractors offers good fishing, particularly for crappie, for which the lake is noted. One of these attractors is located in the long prong of the lake near the dam and is probably the lightest-fished one. Others are located along the northern shore across the lake from the launching ramp.

The fish population is rich and varied. The largemouth bass fishing here is better than in most department lakes. The bluegill fishing is also particularly good. Channel catfish are stocked regularly, and fish up to 10 pounds are there for those who can catch them. Two-pound catfish are taken regularly. In 1989 Lake Orange gave up an unexpected prize. The concession operator was out late one summer day fishing for his dinner table when he landed a 6-pound, 13-ounce white bass, a fish completely foreign to the lake. Following a good bit of consideration, the fish was added to the records as a new world record for white bass. Whether the concession operator ever got to eat his prize catch is unknown, but it created quite a stir in the angling world. No one has any idea how the fish got into the lake. Some angler's live-bait pail? One thing is certain, however. An angler could fish the lake for years targeting white bass and never catch one. The world record was probably the only white bass in the lake.

In the meantime Lake Orange continues to offer good fishing for the more common species.

PHELPS POND

SUPERVISING OFFICE: Department of Game and Inland Fisheries, 1320 Belman Road, Fredericksburg, VA 22401. Telephone (540) 899-4169

LOCATION: Fauquier County

SIZE: 3 acres

DIRECTIONS: From Remington on U.S. 29, the pond is reached by Secondary Route 651, Sumerduck Road. The pond is located near the center of the Phelps Wildlife Management Area. Follow signs to the wildlife management area and take the main entrance, which leads to the manager's residence. Those traveling from the east should take U.S. Highway 17 from Fredericksburg and turn west (or left) on Route 651, Sumerduck Road.

Phelps Pond is located near the middle of the 4,000-acre Phelps Wildlife Management Area, named for the late Chester F. Phelps, longtime director of the Virginia Department of Game and Inland Fisheries. It is approximately 8 miles from Remington, which is on old U.S. Highway 29. The wildlife management area is bordered by several miles of the Rappahannock River, and across the river from the area is the Kelly's Ford access and boat-launching ramp on the river. At only 3 acres, this is certainly one of the smallest bodies of fishable water managed by the department. Viewed from the parking area,

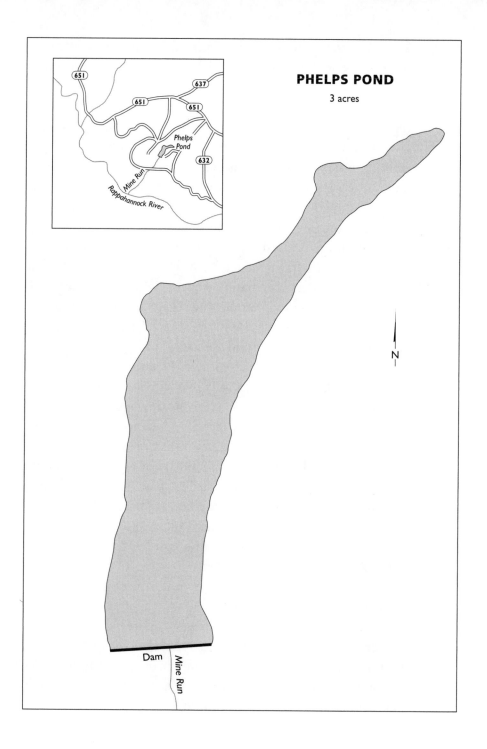

PHELPS POND
3 acres

651
637
651
651
Phelps
Pond
632
Mine Run
Rappahannock River

N

Dam   Mine Run

which is several hundred yards from the pond, it looks much larger, possibly because all of it is not visible. Trees and other vegetation conceal much of it from the casual eye. Much of the near side is open and bordered by a large field, but trees and vegetation line much of the shoreline. On the far side of the pond from the parking area is a mixed pine and hardwood forest that borders the water. It is truly a picturesque little body of water and a joy to fish. The well-marked parking area is near the manager's house and a good walk from the pond. There is no boat-launching ramp on the pond, and most anglers fish from the shore. A good casting or spinning angler can cover most of the lake from the shore. Anglers who desires to fish from a boat or canoe can hand carry the light craft to the pond, but it means a quarter of a mile tote. The craft can be easily slid into the water from the grassy shoreline. There are no docks or other facilities on the pond. Gasoline outboard motors, sailboats, and swimming are prohibited. Electric motors are permitted, but they add to the weight of the long carry. A good paddle provides plenty of power for the tiny body of water.

The fishing opportunities, though good, are limited. Largemouth bass, bluegills, and channel catfish provide most of the fishing, though there are other members of the sunfish family such as the popular redear sunfish. The bass tend to run small, but there are some big fish in the pond. There is a minimum size limit of 18 inches and a creel limit of one fish, but check the fishing regulations posted at the lake for the latest regulations. They may change from time to time. The bluegill fishing is excellent with fish of half a pound common. Fishing for channel catfish can also be good.

On this sprawling wildlife management area along the Rappahannock River, there are ample opportunities for other outdoor activities such as bird-watching, primitive camping, hiking, biking, and, of course, hunting. The wildlife management area is managed primarily for hunting.

LAKE THOMPSON

SUPERVISING OFFICE: Department of Game and Inland Fisheries, 1320 Belman Road, Fredericksburg, VA 22401. Telephone (540) 899-4169

LOCATION: Fauquier County

SIZE: 10 acres

DIRECTIONS: On Interstate 66 west of Marshall, take the Markham or Route 688 exit north onto Secondary Route 688, Leeds Manor Road, and travel north to the second parking area on the left. This is the parking area for Lake Thompson.

This picturesque little mountain lake of only 10 acres is nestled in the foothills of the Blue Ridge Mountains in the G. Richard Thompson Wildlife Management Area. It is one of the smallest of the thirty-two lakes owned and managed specifically for fishing by the Department of Game and Inland Fisheries. Though the lake is rich in a great variety of species of game fish, it is probably most popular as a put-and-take trout fishery. It is classified as Category A trout water, which means it is stocked from October through May. It is also the only water in Fauquier County stocked with trout. It impounds a cold mountain stream and has a lot of deep water, and it probably holds trout all year even though it is not stocked during the warm summer months. From the parking lot anglers must walk several hundred yards up a good incline to reach the lake. At that point there is a small parking lot for handicapped anglers and room for automobiles trailering light boats to turn around and drive back to the main parking lot. There is no launching ramp there, but boats can be slid into the water down a grassy bank. Some anglers obviously back their trailers into the water and unload their boats, but this is unwise. Ideally only canoes and small boats should be launched. Most anglers fish from the shore, which is open just about all around the lake. The dam area is popular among trout anglers during the stocking sea-

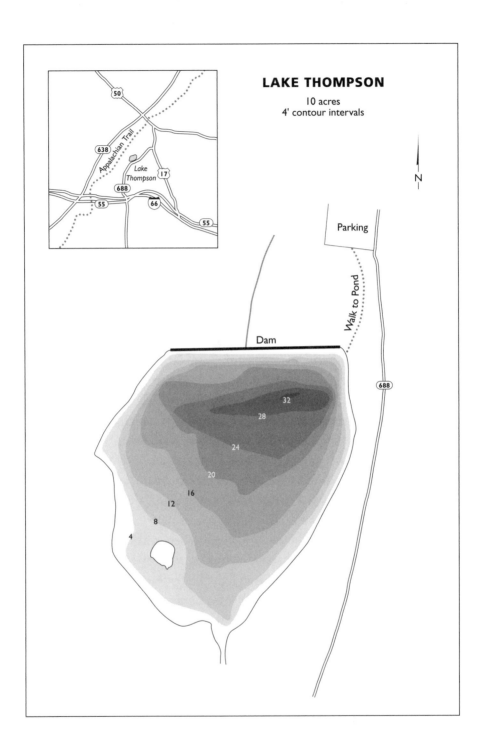

LAKE THOMPSON

10 acres
4' contour intervals

50

638

Appalachian Trail

Lake
Thompson

17

688

55

66

55

N

Parking

Walk to Pond

Dam

688

32

28

24

20

16

12

8

4

son. There are no docks, piers, or other facilities on the lake. The water is deep, ranging from 32 feet or more behind the dam to 4 feet or less in the headwaters or along the shore. Very little of the water is less than 12 to 15 feet deep, however. There is one small island just off the western shoreline.

While the fishing for released trout gets much of the angling attention, there is actually a rich variety of fish in the lake, including bluegills, channel catfish, both brown and rainbow trout, redear sunfish, and smallmouth bass. Some of the smallmouth bass may reach 5 pounds or more. This is the only lake in the region to offer smallmouth bass fishing in an area where the largemouth bass is more abundant. A trout fishing license, in addition to the regular state fishing license, is required during the trout stocking season from October 1 through June 15.

The wildlife management area, of which the lake is an integral part, offers 4,160 acres of the rugged eastern slopes of the Blue Ridge Mountains where hunting, stream fishing for native brook trout, hiking, bird-watching, and primitive camping are all popular outdoor activities. The famous Appalachian Trail is close by. All of this is public land, amazingly convenient to one of the most densely populated areas in America.

6 Other Lakes Managed for Fishing

Multipurpose Waters

This book has been devoted primarily to lakes owned and managed by the Virginia Department of Game and Inland Fisheries for fishing and only fishing as promised in the title. That is its focus. There are thirty-two of them covered in the first five chapters.

There are, however, other lakes or reservoirs in the state, multiple-purpose waters, that serve a great variety of interests. Among them are the big flood-control reservoirs such as Buggs Island Lake, hydroelectric reservoirs such as Smith Mountain Lake, cooling waters for nuclear power generation such as Lake Anna, water-supply lakes such as Chickahominy, the water-recreation lakes in the state parks, and others that also offer good fishing. They too are managed for fishing thanks to agreements between the various interests and the Department of Game and Inland Fisheries. Fishermen, however, must share these waters with boaters, hunters, swimmers, water-skiers, jet boaters, sailboaters, and others who turn to still waters for recreation or other pursuits.

Generally these lakes are considered public water, though in a few instances the owners may place certain restrictions on them.

Probably because they are larger and more prominent, they are often more popular than the department fishing lakes. Collectively they offer many more acres of water, and they also are located throughout Virginia, from the broad coastal plain to the high mountain country to the west and from the Potomac River, which forms the northern border of Virginia, to the North Carolina border. Several like Buggs Island Lake, Gaston, and South Holston are border lakes that straddle the state line.

During the warmer months of the year, anglers have to share these lakes with other users, but during the colder months they often have them pretty much to themselves. Waterfowl hunters may offer some competition on a few of them, but most are large enough to accommodate both anglers and hunters.

Following is a rundown on the major such waters. These are the most popular ones, and all are open to the public for fishing. They are covered here generally according to size, Buggs Island Lake being the largest in the state.

BUGGS ISLAND LAKE

LOCATION: Charlotte, Halifax, and Mecklenburg Counties

SIZE: 50,000 acres

SOURCES OF INFORMATION: Virginia Department of Game and Inland Fisheries, HC 6, Box 46, Farmville, VA 23901. Telephone (434) 392-9645. Virginia Division of Parks and Recreation, 4010 West Broad Street, Richmond, VA 23230-1104. Telephone (804) 367-1000

The 50,000-acre Buggs Island Lake, or John H. Kerr Reservoir, was completed in 1951 and named for a prominent North Carolina congressman who was an early proponent of the lake, its primary purpose being to protect the lower Roanoke River basin from periodic floods. In Virginia, however, it is known as Buggs Island Lake, named for a big island in the Roanoke River, which was impounded to form the lake. It is by far the largest lake in Virginia, twice the size of Lakes Gaston and Smith Mountain, its closest competitors. It straddles the Virginia–North Carolina line. Though the dam is in Virginia, some of the lake is in North Carolina. The water level might vary as much as 25 feet or more because of its flood-control mission. The lake is drawn down 25 feet or more in the fall to make room for floodwaters, but it fills gradually, usually reaching full pool by June.

While the big lake straddles the North Carolina–Virginia border, most of it is in Virginia. The dam and visitors center are in Virginia. A pair of flooded creeks, Grassy and Nutbush, extend the lake deep into North Carolina. U.S. Highway 15 crosses the lake at Clarksville, the major municipality on the lake. Thanks to a long-standing reciprocal agreement between the Virginia Department of Game and Inland Fisheries and the North Carolina Wildlife Resources Commission, fishing licenses of both states are good all over the lake.

Buggs Island Lake is best known for its self-sustaining population of landlocked striped bass. For years before the impounding of the river, the anadromous fish made spawning runs up the Dan and Roanoke Rivers every spring, dropping back into the briny North Carolina waters once their annual mission was completed. When the Roanoke River was impounded, this migration pattern was interrupted, and a good number of the fish were caught upstream. Because they could not return to their native salt water, they took up residence in the giant inland sea created on their spawning river. Soon it became evident that they were continuing their annual spawning migration and reproducing. The word spread quickly, and anglers from all over the region began to travel to Buggs Island Lake for the exciting new kind of striped bass fishing. The Department of Game and Inland Fisheries has since built a striped bass hatchery at Brookneal on the Roanoke River, and biologists are trapping spawning striped bass, stripping them of their eggs, and releasing them. The eggs are then placed in the nearby hatchery, producing fingerling stripers that are released in suitable waters all over the state. In the meantime, fishing for the big fish in Buggs Island Lake continued to grow in popularity. Fishing the Dan and Roanoke Rivers, the major feeder streams of the big lake, during the spawning run is also popular. Public boat-launching ramps on the two rivers facilitate this fishing.

The big lake is also noted for its largemouth bass fishing, with fish in the 2- to 4-pound class fairly common. Crappie also grow large in the lake and are abundant. The white perch population has grown rapidly and apparently has curtailed the growth of the white bass population. The two fish are closely related. Three species of catfish, the blue, channel, and flathead, get a lot of attention. Other species include bluegills and other members of the sunfish family, and an occasional walleye. Chain pickerel are native to the area but do not inhabit large waters. Anglers fish for them in the mouths of many creeks draining into the lake.

Fishing facilities around the lake are excellent, with an abundance of public boat-launching ramps installed by the Department of Game and Inland Fisheries, the North Carolina Wildlife Commission, the U.S. Corps of Engineers, and the Virginia Division of Parks and Recreation. A number of ramps owned and operated by marinas also are available for a modest fee. Professional fishing guides also work the lake.

LAKE GASTON

LOCATION: Brunswick and Mecklenburg Counties

SIZE: 20,600 acres

SOURCE OF INFORMATION: Virginia Department of Game and Inland Fisheries, HC 6, Box 46, Farmville, VA 23901. Telephone (434) 392-9645

Also located on the Roanoke River, the headwaters of Lake Gaston back up against the John H. Kerr Dam. It is owned by the Dominion Virginia Power Company for the production of hydroelectric power. By law the water level in Lake Gaston must be maintained at full pool by releases from Buggs Island Lake. For that reason, the water level is constant. Much of the lake is in North Carolina, but thanks to a reciprocal agreement between the Virginia Department of Game and Inland Fisheries and the North Carolina Wildlife Commission, licensed anglers of both states can fish the entire lake.

Lake Gaston is noted for its excellent largemouth bass fishing. Many anglers like to fish the rich aquatic vegetation, and the constant water level favors this kind of fishing. The North Carolina Wildlife Commission stocks the lake frequently with striped bass. Fishing for the silvery fish in the tail waters below Kerr Dam draws anglers every spring as the fish attempt to move upstream on their annual spawning ritual. While the North Carolina Wildlife Commission fisheries managers maintain the striped bass fishing, biologists of the Virginia Department of Game and Inland Fisheries maintain a walleye population with annual releases of the fish. The walleye fishing is usually best in the upper reaches of the lake during February and March. In addition to largemouth bass, striped bass, and walleyes, anglers will also find bluegills, blue and channel catfish, chain pickerel, and crappie.

Both the Virginia Department of Game and Inland Fisheries and the North Carolina Wildlife Commission maintain boat-launching ramps at convenient locations around the lake. Professional fishing guides also work the lake.

SMITH MOUNTAIN AND LEESVILLE LAKES

LOCATION: Bedford, Campbell, Franklin, and Pittsylvania Counties

SIZE: 20,600 and 3,400 acres

SOURCE OF INFORMATION: Virginia Department of Game and Inland Fisheries, 1132 Thomas Jefferson Drive, Forest, VA 24551. Telephone (434) 525-7522

The Smith Mountain and Leesville complex on the Roanoke River was completed in 1966 and began generating electricity. A project of the American Electric Power Company, it is a pumped-storage hydroelectric power complex. The water, generating power as it passes through the Smith Mountain Lake dam into Leesville Lake immediately downstream, is then pumped back into the upper lake to be used again. As a consequence, there is very little fluctuation in the upper lake, the more popular fishing lake of the two. Smith Mountain could well be the most popular fishing lake in Virginia because of its excellent striped bass fishing. It has also produced a couple of record muskies and is noted for its big crappie. Other angling possibilities include catfish, both largemouth and smallmouth bass, a variety of sunfish including big bluegills, walleye, white bass, and yellow perch.

Fishing in Leesville Lake suffers from the constant fluctuation of the water level, but it offers some good walleye fishing, which is maintained by annual stocking on the part of the Department of Game and Inland Fisheries. The striped bass fishing is good, and the white bass average a pound. Other possibilities include both largemouth and smallmouth bass, crappie, and a variety of sunfish.

The Department of Game and Inland Fisheries maintains a number of boat-launching ramps on Smith Mountain Lake and several on the smaller Leesville Lake. Numerous marinas also offer access to Smith Mountain Lake, and the Smith Mountain Lake State Park boat ramp has a handicapped-accessible fishing pier. There is also a public catwalk below the Leesville Lake dam, but when using it, keep an ear peeled for a siren which signals that water is being released through the Smith Mountain Lake dam and could flood the catwalk. A number of professional fishing guides work Smith Mountain Lake.

LAKE ANNA

LOCATION: Louisa, Orange, and Spotsylvania Counties

SIZE: 13,000 acres

SOURCE OF INFORMATION: Virginia Department of Game and Inland Fisheries, 1320 Belman Road, Fredericksburg, VA 22401. Telephone (540) 899-4169

Impounded in 1972 on the North Anna River to provide cooling water for the North Anna nuclear power plant, Lake Anna is the newest of the large reservoirs or lakes in Virginia. Located convenient to the population centers of Richmond and Northern Virginia, it is also one of the most popular lakes. Despite the fishing pressure it is subjected to, the fishing remains good. There are actually two bodies of water here, the main lake of 9,600 acres and the smaller cooling pond, fondly referred to as the "hot side." It is owned by the Dominion Virginia Power Company. There is a handicapped-accessible catwalk for anglers at dike 3 where warm water from the cooling pond enters the lake and attracts fish during the winter months. The Department of Game and Inland Fisheries, Dominion Virginia Power Company, and local anglers and fishing guides have placed a number of fish attractors throughout the lake. They are well marked and should receive the attention of anglers. They hold a variety of fish. Largemouth bass, striped bass, and crappie receive the lion's share of the angling attention, but the bluegill and redear sunfish populations are also strong. The white perch fishing is good during the winter months. Fishermen also take an occasional catfish, chain pickerel, and yellow perch. The variety is rich.

The only public boat-launching ramp is located in the Lake Anna State Park, and there is a fee for using it. There is no other public access to the lake, but numerous marinas around the lake offer launching facilities for a modest fee. Lake Anna State Park is located on the lake.

SOUTH HOLSTON LAKE

LOCATION: Washington County

SIZE: 7,580 acres

SOURCE OF INFORMATION: Virginia Department of Game and Inland Fisheries, 1796 Highway Sixteen, Marion, VA 24354. Telephone (276) 783-4860

South Holston Lake is a Tennessee Valley Authority project on the Virginia-Tennessee border, but much of the lake is in Virginia, approximately 1,600 acres. Unfortunately the Virginia Department of Game and Inland Fisheries and the Tennessee Wildlife Resources Agency have not been able to reach a reciprocal agreement that would open the entire lake to licensed anglers of both states. Virginia anglers need a Tennessee license to fish the Tennessee portion of the lake, the larger portion. And Tennessee regulations apply there. Pick up a copy of the Tennessee regulations when purchasing a license, available at marinas on the Tennessee shores of the lake. Fishing for smallmouth bass might well be the top fishing in this deep reservoir on the South Holston River, which rises in Virginia and flows into Tennessee. The largemouth bass fishing is also good and often overlooked. The walleye and crappie fishing are good, with many crappie in the 10- to 12-inch range. Tennessee fisheries managers also stock rainbow trout in the lake, and the best fishing for them is in deep Tennessee waters near the dam. Various members of the sunfish family including bluegills and redear sunfish are abundant. Also finning the waters are both channel and flathead catfish and white bass.

There is one public boat-launching ramp near the headwaters of the lake. There is also a boat-launching ramp in Washington County Park, but a modest fee is exacted. Several marinas also offer launching facilities for a fee.

CLAYTOR LAKE

LOCATION: Pulaski County

SIZE: 4,475 acres

SOURCE OF INFORMATION: Virginia Department of Game and Inland Fisheries, Draper Aden Building, 2206 South Main Street, Suite C, Blacksburg, VA 24060. Telephone (540) 951-7923

Claytor Lake, an American Electric Power Company hydro-electric reservoir, is one of the oldest large lakes in Virginia. It is a major impoundment on the New River. The Claytor Lake State Park is located on its shores and draws campers from all over Virginia. The long, narrow lake in the New River basin is probably the only large lake in Virginia that can claim all three black bass, the largemouth, smallmouth, and the smaller spotted bass. The smallmouth, however, is the most abundant. The largemouth creel is rarely large. Nor is that of the spotted bass, which rarely goes over 2 pounds. Striped bass are stocked annually, and the fishing is best during the colder months, which is generally true of all striper lakes. Hybrid striped bass also have been introduced to the lake and are popular among anglers because they are hard fighters. Walleyes and white bass are present but not in an abundance. Crappie tend to run small, but bluegills up to a half pound are popular among anglers. Both channel and flathead catfish up to 20 pounds fin the clear waters of the lake, and yellow perch of a pound or more turn up in the creels of many anglers.

The Department of Game and Inland Fisheries maintains several boat-launching ramps at convenient locations on the lake, and there is also a ramp in Claytor Lake State Park. Several marinas also offer launching facilities for a modest fee.

LAKE CHESDIN

LOCATION: Amelia, Chesterfield, and Dinwiddie Counties

SIZE: 3,060 acres

SOURCE OF INFORMATION: Virginia Department of Game and Inland Fisheries, 4010 West Broad Street, Richmond, VA 23230-1104. Telephone (804) 367-1000

Lake Chesdin on the Appomattox River is owned and managed by the Appomattox River Authority. Lake Chesdin is one of a few lakes to offer fishing for both black and white crappie, and the slab-sided fish grow big. The largemouth bass fishing is also superb, and walleyes grow to 8 pounds or more. The big bluegills attract many anglers, and there is a good population of large channel catfish. The Department of Game and Inland Fisheries periodically releases both striped bass and walleye fingerlings. A few hybrid striped bass remain from previous releases, but they are no longer stocked in this popular long and narrow flat country lake.

The Department of Game and Inland Fisheries owns and maintains a public boat-launching ramp in the vicinity of the dam.

PHILPOTT LAKE

LOCATION: Franklin, Henry, and Patrick Counties

SIZE: 2,800 acres

SOURCE OF INFORMATION: Virginia Department of Game and Inland Fisheries, 1132 Thomas Jefferson Drive, Forest, VA 24551. Telephone (434) 525-7522

Philpott is a deep mountain lake along the eastern slopes of the Blue Ridge Mountains. Its steep shoreline leaves little room for shallow water, making it a difficult lake to fish. It is a flood-control and hydroelectric project of the U.S. Army Corps of Engineers on the Smith River. Fairystone State Park with campgrounds and a small lake of its own is nearby. Philpott is a trout lake, with both brown and rainbow trout being stocked annually, but they are difficult to catch in the deep, clear water. Largemouth and smallmouth bass and walleyes attract most anglers. Other possibilities include channel catfish, crappie, and several members of the sunfish family, including some big bluegills.

The U.S. Army Corps of Engineers offers campgrounds and convenient boat access points and launching ramps all around the lake.

LAKE MOOMAW

LOCATION: Alleghany and Bath Counties

SIZE: 2,530 acres

SOURCE OF INFORMATION: Virginia Department of Game and Inland Fisheries, P.O. Box 996, Verona, VA 24482. Telephone (540) 248-9360

This flood-control reservoir was completed in 1981 by the U.S. Army Corps of Engineers, a 12-mile-long mountain lake on the Jackson River upstream from Covington. As is typical of flood-control lakes, the water level is drawn down 15 feet or more in late summer. The George Washington National Forest supervises most recreation facilities such as campgrounds, picnic areas, and boat-launching ramps.

The lake is probably best known for its excellent trout fishing and big yellow perch, for which it has set several state records. The introduced brown trout grow rapidly, attaining weights of 2 to 3 pounds in a couple of growing seasons. Also highly successful has been the introduction of McConaughty rainbow trout, which make runs up the Jackson River during winter and early spring. The fishing for both largemouth and smallmouth bass is good, and chain pickerel, native to the Jackson River, are abundant. Crappie fishing is good, with fish of a pound or more fairly common. The channel cat fishing is good, and there are strong populations of bluegills and redear sunfish. Moomaw within a span of a very few years has become one of Virginia's most popular fishing destinations.

There are several boat-launching ramps for which a modest fee is exacted.

OCCOQUAN LAKE

LOCATION: Fairfax and Prince William Counties

SIZE: 2,300 acres

SOURCE OF INFORMATION: Virginia Department of Game and Inland Fisheries, 1320 Belman Road, Fredericksburg, VA 22401. Telephone (540) 899-4169

Occoquan Lake, an impoundment on the Occoquan River, is a water-supply reservoir for the Fairfax County Water Authority. Most of the long, narrow lake is within the riverbed, and its banks are steep. It was once noted for its northern pike fish, but the big pike are no longer stocked by the Department of Game and Inland Fisheries. In recent years, however, it has developed a reputation for its big largemouth bass. One survey made by the department biologists indicated that more than 60 percent of the adult population of bass were over 15 inches in length. Alewives and gizzard shad are abundant and provide a rich forage-fish population for the bass. There are also good populations of bluegills, channel catfish, both black and white crappie, channel and flathead catfish, walleye, and white perch. A 66-pound, 4-ounce flathead catfish taken from the lake set a new state record.

Gasoline outboard motors are permitted, but they can be no larger than 10 horsepower. There are no public boat-launching ramps on the lake, but a pair of marinas offer launching ramps and rental boats.

DIASCUND LAKE

LOCATION: James City and New Kent Counties

SIZE: 1,700 acres

SOURCE OF INFORMATION: Virginia Department of Game and Inland Fisheries, 5806 Mooretown Road, Williamsburg, VA 23188. Telephone (757) 253-7072

Diascund Lake is a water-supply reservoir for the city of Newport News and is open to fishing during daylight hours only—from an hour before sunrise until an hour after sunset. The lake is noted for its jumbo chain pickerel and bowfin. It also can be productive of good fishing for largemouth bass. Gizzard shad and blueback herring are the most abundant forage fish for the bass and chain pickerel. The bluegill population, fish in 7- to 8-inch lengths, is also strong. Other possibilities include black crappie; redear sunfish, better known as shellcrackers; and white and yellow perch.

There is a public boat ramp and courtesy pier, and bank fishing is allowed in designated areas in the vicinity of the boat ramp. Electric motors only are permitted. No gasoline outboard motors in this water-supply reservoir.

WESTERN BRANCH LAKE

LOCATION: City of Suffolk

SIZE: 1,579 acres

SOURCE OF INFORMATION: Virginia Department of Game and Inland Fisheries, Deep Creek, 3909 Airline Boulevard, Chesapeake, VA 23321. Telephone (757) 465-6811

Western Branch is the largest of the popular Suffolk Lakes, lakes located in the city of Suffolk. There is a cluster of five of these lakes, all water-supply reservoirs for the tidewater cities of Norfolk and Portsmouth. To fish them the angler needs a permit from the cities that own them. Western Branch is by far the largest, the others being in the 500-acre range, but all are productive fishing waters that together offer good fishing for a great variety of warmwater fish. Located on the western branch of the Nansemond River, the lake is formed in the shape of a horseshoe. Upstream on one of the forks is Lake Burnt Mills and on the other Lake Prince, both members of the Suffolk Lakes cluster. The lake is open all year and usually free of ice in this extreme eastern part of Virginia. The winter fishing can be good.

Back in the 1960s Western Branch was considered one of the best chain pickerel lakes in Virginia, but the heavy stocking of other fish by the Department of Game and Inland Fisheries has forced a lesser role on this popular member of the pike family. Of the twenty-two species for which the department offers citations, thirteen are found in this lake. It is one of the top lakes in the state for trophy bluegills and other sunfish, primarily redear sunfish; largemouth bass; and both white and yellow perch. Striped bass have been introduced and are doing well. Muskie have also been introduced but in very limited numbers. There is always the possibility of tying into one of these big trophy fish.

Gasoline outboard motors up to 12 horsepower are permitted, and there is a boat ramp. The lake is open to fishing from sunrise to sunset, and banking fishing is permitted in an area near the concession and fishing station.

CHICKAHOMINY LAKE

LOCATION: Charles City and New Kent Counties

SIZE: 1,300 acres

SOURCE OF INFORMATION: Virginia Department of Game and Inland Fisheries, 5806 Mooretown Road, Willamsburg, VA 23188. Telephone (757) 253-7072

The Chickahominy Lake on the Chickahominy River is a water-supply reservoir for the city of Newport News. A low dam, known as Walker's Dam, forms the long, narrow lake, much of which is within the banks of the river. The river was impounded in 1943, and twin Denil fish ladders were installed to allow the passage of popular anadromous fish such as herring and striped bass. The dam is on the fall line that separates the jurisdiction of the Department of Game and Inland Fisheries and the Virginia Marine Resources Commission. Different fishing regulations apply above and below the dam, particularly with respect to anadromous fish. Located a short distance from Richmond, the lake has been popular among anglers for over half a century.

The habitat for fish is rich and varied, including cypress trees, submerged aquatic vegetation, and water lilies. In fact, the thick aquatic vegetation, though good for the fish, makes operating an outboard motor difficult. The lake is surrounded by marshes, and its water is acid-stained but fertile.

The largemouth bass fishing has been good in the lake for years, and big chain pickerel enrich most bass creels. They are abundant in the lake. Frequently the lake has ranked first in the state for the production of chain pickerel. The rich fish population includes bluegills, channel catfish, crappie, redear sunfish, striped bass, warmouth, and white and yellow perch.

There are no public boat-launching ramps on the lake, but several very active marinas provide launching facilities at a modest fee, as well as rental boats.

JOHN W. FLANNAGAN LAKE

LOCATION: Dickenson County

SIZE: 1,400 acres

SOURCE OF INFORMATION: Virginia Department of Game and Inland Fisheries, 1796 Highway Sixteen, Marion, VA 24354. Telephone (276) 783-4860

John W. Flannagan is a deep mountain lake, an impoundment on the Pound River, and was built by the U.S. Army Corps of Engineers for flood control. It has steep shorelines that pitch into the water, long and narrow with water that is extremely clear during the summer and fall. This is a popular vacation spot thanks to several developed campgrounds maintained by the U.S. Army Corps of Engineers. There is also primitive camping in the Jefferson National Forest.

Hybrid striped bass first introduced in 1999 continue to provide excellent fishing, and the fish are stocked annually to maintain the popular fishery. The lake also offers good fishing for both largemouth and smallmouth bass. Walleyes are also being released annually and provide good fishing. The popular fish make annual spawning runs up the Pound and Cranesnest Rivers. There is a 10-inch minimum size limit on crappie, which speaks for the quality of the fishing. The Department of Game and Inland Fisheries stocks adult-size fish each year, hoping to increase the population of spawning crappie. Channel and flat-head catfish of trophy size are common. Both muskie and trout have been stocked in the past, and a few lingering fish continue to show up in anglers' creels.

Several Corps of Engineers access points and boat-launching ramps provide quick access to the lake.

LITTLE CREEK RESERVOIR

LOCATION: James City County

SIZE: 947 acres

SOURCES OF INFORMATION: Virginia Department of Game and Inland Fisheries, 5806 Mooretown Road, Williamsburg, VA 23188. Telephone (757) 253-7072. Or call the lake concession at (757)566-1702. It is administered by James City County.

This fertile fishing lake is part of the city of Newport News water supply. The lake is relatively deep and clear with limited structure. The best fishing is along points and at drop-offs. The angler will find a depth finder extremely helpful. Gasoline-powered outboard motors are prohibited, but electric motors are popular.

The lake has an excellent population of largemouth bass. There are also excellent populations of chain pickerel, crappie, redear sunfish, and yellow perch. There are both blue and channel catfish up to 25 pounds, an average bluegill population, and a developing striped bass population. The fishing is obviously good.

There is a boat-launching ramp and a free fishing pier. Boats, canoes, and electric motors can be rented at the concession.

LAKE MANASSAS

LOCATION: Prince William County

SIZE: 800 acres

SOURCE OF INFORMATION: Virginia Department of Game and Inland Fisheries, 1320 Belman Road, Fredericksburg, VA 22401. Telephone (540) 899-4169

Lake Manassas is part of the water supply for the city of Manassas. A recent increase in the lake's normal pool flooded shoreline brush and timber, creating excellent additional cover for the rich fish population. It is an impoundment on Broad Run, a popular Northern Virginia stream that anglers from the area have turned to over the years.

There are good populations of both largemouth bass and walleyes, and some smallmouth bass fishing in the Broad Run arm of the lake. Channel catfish are also abundant in this suburban lake. The spring fishing is good for crappie, both black and white.

The lake is surrounded by the development of town houses and apartments. There is also a golf course on its shores. While the lake is open to public fishing, access is not good, but that is being addressed.

LAKE PRINCE

LOCATION: City of Suffolk

SIZE: 777 acres

SOURCE OF INFORMATION: Virginia Department of Game and Inland Fisheries, Deep Creek, 3909 Airline Boulevard, Chesapeake, VA 23321. Telephone (757) 465-6811

One of the Suffolk Lakes, a cluster of lakes in the city of Suffolk, Lake Prince is also one of the older lakes in the city of Norfolk's water-supply system. It was impounded in 1925 and has been a popular fishing spot for years. A fishing permit is needed from the city of Norfolk but is usually available at the Lake Prince fishing station. It is a deep lake up to 30 feet, and it has numerous deep coves. The lake is fed by cypress-tree-studded Carbell and Ennis Swamps.

The striped bass population is excellent, with fish being stocked annually. An aeration system installed during the early 1990s is believed to have improved the survival of the popular fishing during the hot summer weather the lake is subjected to. A few trophy stripers are landed every fishing season. The lake is also home to a good population of largemouth bass and redear sunfish. Bluegill numbers are high, and there are good populations of black crappie and chain pickerel. Most species of game fish can be caught all year, but the cooler months are best for the big members of the pike family.

There is a boat ramp at the Lake Prince fishing station, and gasoline-powered outboard motors of up to 12 horsepower are permitted. Bank fishing is restricted to a small area near the fishing station. Fishing hours are sunrise until sunset.

SANDY RIVER RESERVOIR

LOCATION: Prince Edward County

SIZE: 740 acres

SOURCES OF INFORMATION: Virginia Department of Game and Inland Fisheries, HC 6, Box 46, Farmville, VA 24060. Telephone (434) 392-9645. Or Prince Edward County, telephone (434) 392-8837

This water-supply reservoir for Prince Edward County is one of Virginia's newest fishing lakes, and a productive one. The Prince Edward County Board of Supervisors liberalized regulations to allow fishing 24 hours a day. This increases angling opportunities for catfish and walleyes, both of which have been stocked in the lake. Catfish and walleye fishing is often best after dark. Prohibited activities include alcohol use, camping, jet skies, littering, seining, swimming, and trotlines, prohibitions which add to the joy of a quiet day of fishing on a spectacular lake. Regulations are conspicuously posted and should be consulted before kicking off a fishing trip. A double-lane boat-launching ramp, a courtesy pier, and a 150-foot handicapped-accessible fishing pier are the products of a cooperative effort on the part of the Department of Game and Inland Fisheries, the Prince Edward County Board of Supervisors, Dominion Virginia Power Company, and the Virginia National Guard. Also installed around the fishing pier are fish attractors to enhance the habitat. Gasoline-powered outboard motors up to 10 horsepower are permitted, enabling anglers to reach the productive upper reaches of the lake quickly.

The lake offers a wide population of largemouth bass, bluegills, crappie, and redear sunfish, or shellcrackers as they are better known. Channel catfish have been introduced and offer angling promise. Walleyes have also been stocked, unsuccessfully earlier but doubling the number of fish stocked has improved the fishing for this popular fish. There are also good populations of native fish, primarily chain pickerel and bullhead catfish.

LUNGA RESERVOIR

LOCATION: Stafford County

SIZE: 670 acres

SOURCE OF INFORMATION: U.S. Marine Corps Base at Quantico, Quantico, VA 22134. Telephone (703) 784-5383

Lunga Reservoir is the largest of six small lakes and ponds on the Marine Corps Reservation at Quantico, Virginia. Others range in size from an acre upward. A fishing permit available from the base authorities is required to fish these waters. These various lakes are fed by Beaver Dam and Flat Runs, Cannon Creek, and South Branch. The U.S. Marine Corps and the U.S. Fish and Wildlife Service manage these public fishing waters.

Abundant in a mixed fish population are white perch and walleyes. There are also some big bullhead catfish averaging 16 inches in length.

BEAVERDAM SWAMP RESERVOIR

LOCATION: Gloucester County

SIZE: 635 acres

SOURCES OF INFORMATION: Virginia Department of Game and Inland Fisheries, 5806 Mooretown Road, Williamsburg, VA 23188. Telephone (757) 253-7072. Or Gloucester Parks and Recreation Department, (804) 693-2355, or the concession, (804) 693-2107

This water-supply reservoir is located just outside Gloucester, the county seat of Gloucester County. In addition to fishing opportunities, the area also offers biking, hiking, and riding trails and picnic facilities. The lake is filled with standing timber, submerged aquatic vegetation, and fish attractors, all of which provide excellent habitat for a healthy and mixed fish population.

The fishing for largemouth bass, black crappie, channel catfish, and redear sunfish is excellent. The bass population is in good shape in terms of abundance and size. Fish in excess of 15 inches are common, and larger ones fin the waters of the lake. The crappie population is also strong, with most fish exceeding 8 inches in length and many over 12 inches. A good portion of the channel catfish population is greater than 24 inches long.

There are a pair of boat-launching ramps available upon the purchase of daily or annual permits. There is no charge for bank fishing, and a fishing pier is available. Gasoline-powered outboard motors are prohibited, but electric motors are permitted. Boats and canoes are available for renting.

BURNT MILLS LAKE

LOCATION: City of Suffolk and Isle of Wight County

SIZE: 610 acres

SOURCE OF INFORMATION: Virginia Department of Game and Inland Fisheries, Deep Creek, 3909 Airline Boulevard, Chesapeake, VA 23321. Telephone (757) 465-6811

Burnt Mills Lake, one of the cluster of Suffolk Lakes, is part of the water-supply system of the city of Norfolk. An old lake, it was impounded back in the early 1940s. A deep lake with depths up to 50 feet, its major source of water is the Great Swamp, a dense cypress swamp. The upper half of the lake is filled with stumps and should be navigated with care. Gasoline-powered outboard motors up to 12 horsepower are permitted. Bank fishing is prohibited. To fish the lake a city permit available at the fishing station is required.

Surveys of the lake made by fisheries biologists indicate a good population of largemouth bass, black crappie, bluegills, catfish, chain pickerel, redear sunfish, or shellcrackers, and yellow perch. Over the years it has enjoyed a reputation for giving up trophy bluegills.

There is an undeveloped boat ramp and an automobile and trailer parking area near the dam.

LAKE MEADE

LOCATION: City of Suffolk

SIZE: 512 acres

SOURCES OF INFORMATION: Virginia Department of Game and Inland Fisheries, Deep Creek, 3909 Airline Boulevard, Chesapeake, VA 23321. Telephone (757) 465-6811. Or call Cohoon-Meade Fishing Station, (757) 539-6216

Lake Meade is one of the youngest reservoirs in the city of Portsmouth water-supply system, having been impounded in 1960 on the main stem of the Nansemond River. It is a horseshoe-shaped body of water with Lake Kilby on one arm and Lake Cohoon on the other. It has a maximum depth of approximately 25 feet. Fishing permits from the city are required, and they are available at the Cohoon-Meade Fishing Station.

The lake holds a rich variety of fish. It is stocked annually with striped bass. Also present are good populations of largemouth bass, bluegills, catfish, chain pickerel, crappie, redear sunfish, and white and yellow perch. Other members of the big sunfish family include fliers and warmouth, fish of the swamp drainage.

The Cohoon-Meade Fishing Station offers a paved boat-launching ramp, rental boats, and limited fishing tackle. Gasoline-powered outboard motors are limited to 10 horsepower or less.

LAKE COHOON

LOCATION: City of Suffolk

SIZE: 510 acres

SOURCES OF INFORMATION: Virginia Department of Game and Inland Fisheries, Deep Creek, 3909 Airline Boulevard, Chesapeake, VA 23321. Telephone (757) 465-6811. Or Cohoon-Meade Fishing Station, (757) 539-6216

Lake Cohoon is a part of the city of Portsmouth water-supply system. A permit available at the Cohoon-Meade Fishing Station is required to fish the lake. The permit, however, is good for all four lakes in the city water supply, Cohoon, Kilby, Meade, and Speight's Run. Cohoon is a relatively shallow coastal-plain lake with a maximum depth of approximately 30 feet. There are numerous coves in the lake that should get the angler's attention.

Fishing is excellent for largemouth bass, bluegills, chain pickerel, crappie, and redear sunfish. The lake is a top producer of big chain pickerel, giving up several 6-pounders every fishing season. The lake is also noted for its trophy crappie and has been stocked with walleye.

The fishing facilities are good, with the fishing station offering a concrete boat-launching ramp, rental boats, bait, limited fishing tackle, and snacks. The concession is open seven days a week during the warm fishing season but usually only on weekends during the winter. The ramp, of course, is open all year. Gasoline-powered outboard motors are limited to 10 horsepower or smaller. Bank fishing is limited to the area adjacent to the fishing station. Fishing from the dam is prohibited.

LAKE WHITEHURST

LOCATION: City of Norfolk and City of Virginia Beach

SIZE: 458 acres

SOURCES OF INFORMATION: Virginia Department of Game and Inland Fisheries, Deep Creek, 3909 Airline Boulevard, Chesapeake, VA 23321. Telephone (757) 465-6811. Or Lake Smith Fishing Station, (757) 587-1755

Lake Whitehurst is part of the water-supply system for the city of Norfolk. It is a divided lake separated by U.S. Highway 13, or Northampton Boulevard, which crosses it. The two sections are connected by a narrow canal which is impassable by boat because of low overhanging pipes. One section, also known as Little Creek Reservoir, is located in Virginia Beach and is very shallow, not over 6 feet at its deepest point. The other section, which contains a large number of deep pits that provide depths of up to 40 feet, offers the best habitat, particularly for walleyes during the hot summer months. This lowlands lake is fed primarily by swamps.

The lake hosts a rich variety of fish and possibly is the best walleye-fishing lake in Virginia. At least it produces the elusive walleye more consistently than most other Virginia lakes. Many fish are in the 4- to 6-pound class, a good walleye. The winter fishing is good, with many fish being caught by jigging. While anglers catch walleyes all year, the best fishing is in the spring months. A good spot to catch the fish at this season is below the box culvert beneath Northampton Boulevard where the fish attempt spawning runs upstream. The black crappie and white perch populations are strong, with fish of over a pound fairly common. There is a fair population of largemouth bass, and those taken by anglers are usually fairly large. Other fish include bluegills, catfish, chain pickerel, redear sunfish, and yellow perch.

A permit from the city of Norfolk is needed to put a boat on the lake, and gasoline-powered outboard motors up to 12 horsepower are permitted. There is an unimproved boat ramp on the Little Creek Reservoir side of the lake and a pair of concrete boat-launching ramps on Lake Whitehurst. Bank fishing is limited to a pair of fishing piers, both handicapped accessible. There is also a concession on Lake Whitehurst which offers rental boats, limited fishing tackle, and snacks.

LEE HALL LAKE

LOCATION: City of Newport News

SIZE: 492 acres

SOURCES OF INFORMATION: Virginia Department of Game and Inland Fisheries, Deep Creek, 3909 Airline Boulevard, Chesapeake, VA 23321. Telephone (757) 465-6811. And Newport News Department of Parks and Recreation, (757) 886-7912

Lee Hall Lake, also known as the Newport News City Reservoir, is part of the Newport News water-supply system, but it is open to public fishing. A shallow coastal-plains lake surrounded by forests, it is located in the Newport News City Park. The lake is divided into the upper and middle basins by Interstate Highway 64, which crosses the lake. Both sides of the lake are visible to travelers on the highway. The lower basin, from which water for a water-treatment plant is taken, is closed to fishing. The park is a favorite for family recreation, offering campgrounds, nature trails, picnic shelters, and boat rentals.

There are good populations of largemouth bass, chain pickerel, and redear sunfish. Also finning its fertile waters are bluegills, crappie, and white and yellow perch. Channel catfish are stocked periodically. Stocking of northern pike has been discontinued, but there maybe remnant populations.

There is a boat ramp for which a small fee is exacted. Daily or annual permits to use the ramp are available. There is limited bank fishing. Gasoline-powered outboard motors are prohibited, but electric motors are allowed.

RIVANNA RESERVOIR

LOCATION: Albemarle County

SIZE: 450 acres

SOURCE OF INFORMATION: Virginia Department of Game

and Inland Fisheries, 4010 West Broad Street, Richmond, VA 23230-1104. Telephone (804) 367-1000

The Rivanna Reservoir is part of the water-supply system for the city of Charlottesville. It is a long, reasonably deep mountain lake, mostly within the riverbed of the South Fork of the Rivanna River, which it impounds. Feeder streams include Ivy Branch and the Mechums and Moormans Rivers. The lake is open to fishing from sunrise to sunset. The dam is visible just upstream from the U.S. Highway 29 bridge over the South Fork of the Rivanna River just north of Charlottesville.

The locally popular lake is noted for its crappie fishing and an outstanding population of channel catfish, many in the 5-pound or larger range. Largemouth bass are abundant, and walleyes grow to 3 to 5 pounds. Other species in a rich population include bluegills, pumpkinseed sunfish, and redear sunfish, or shellcrackers.

There is a lone boat-launching ramp downlake near the dam, but parking space for vehicles and boat trailers is limited. Gasoline-powered outboard motors are prohibited, but electric motors are popular.

Virginia State Park Lakes

A number of Virginia state parks contain lakes or ponds, mostly small but still productive for fishing. These are primarily recreation lakes, of course, with swimming beaches, boat rentals including canoes and paddleboats, and campgrounds often on the shores of the lake. For example, if an angler can get a campsite on the shores of Douthat Lake near Clifton Forge, he can launch his private boat or canoe or rent one from the park and enjoy a real fishing vacation while his family swims, suns on the sandy beach, enjoys evening programs, and hikes one of several trails. The boat can be pulled on the shore near the campsite, always ready to go for an hour or two of fishing. Most parks have rental boats or canoes and often a limited supply of fishing tackle for sale.

These small bodies of water are managed by the Department of Game and Inland Fisheries and productive of good fishing for a variety of fish.

They are listed here in alphabetical order.

BEAR CREEK LAKE

Bear Creek Lake is located in Bear Creek Lake State Park in Cumberland County. It is a 42-acre lake that offers fishing for largemouth bass, bluegills, channel catfish, and crappie. The lake is situated near the heart of Cumberland State Forest and was built in 1938 as a project of the State Forestry Division. It was given to the Division of State Forests in 1940. Facilities include a handicapped-accessible fishing pier and facilities for launching cartop boats. Rowboats and canoes are available for renting. Gasoline-powered outboard motors are prohibited, but electric motors are permitted. For information, contact Bear Creek State Park, Route 1, Box 253, Cumberland, VA 23040, telephone (804) 492-4410, or the Virginia Division of Parks and Recreation at the address given below.

DOUTHAT LAKE

Fifty-acre Douthat Lake in the Douthat State Park in Alleghany and Bath Counties is probably best known among anglers for its fine fee-fishing trout program. From April through June and from September through October, it is stocked twice a week with brook, brown, and rainbow trout, and anglers are charged a modest fee to fish the lake. In addition to the stocked trout, the lake provides good fishing for largemouth bass, black crappie, bluegills and other sunfish, and channel catfish. It also has an excellent native chain pickerel population and has produced several state records. There are two fishing piers and a gravel boat-launching ramp for private boats. Fish attractors have been installed near the piers. Rental boats are available most of the year. Additional information is available by calling the park at (540) 862-8100 or contacting the Virginia Division of Parks and Recreation at the address given below.

FAIRYSTONE LAKE

Fairystone Lake is located in Fairystone State Park in Patrick County. At 168 acres Fairystone Lake is one of the largest in the state park system. This attractive lake has many deep coves an angler can explore. Additionally, park personnel have built a number of fish shelters and sunk them in the lake. The lake has a good population of largemouth bass in the 12- to 15-inch range, plus bluegills, crappie, and redear sunfish, or shellcrackers. The panfish, however, tend to run small. Channel catfish are stocked periodically. There are rental boats, including both johnboats and canoes, and there is a gravel boat ramp where private boats can be launched. For further information, contact the park at (276) 930-3927 or the Division of Parks and Recreation at the address given below.

HOLIDAY LAKE

Holiday Lake in the Holiday Lake State Park in Appomattox County is, at 150 acres, one of the largest lakes in the state parks system. The park is surrounded by the Buckingham-Appomattox State Forest. The lake is clear and not overly productive of fish populations, but it supports a good largemouth bass population and is probably best known for its chain pickerel fishing, being located in the heart of good chain pickerel country. The fish are native to the area and live in the stream feeding into the lake. Black crappies also provide good fishing, and the bluegill and other sunfish population offers good fishing for panfish. The lake is usually clear and sparkles in a delightful setting surrounded by forest lands. There are good opportunities for bank fishing, and there are rental boats and a gravel boat-launching ramp. For further information, call the park at (434) 248-6303 or contact the Virginia Division of Parks and Recreation at the address below.

HUNGRY MOTHER STATE PARK

Hungry Mother Lake in the Hungry Mother State Park is beyond question the best fishing lake in the state park system based on the rich variety of fish. It is a 108-acre picturesque mountain lake and a joy to be on. Finning its clear waters are largemouth, smallmouth, and spotted bass. Very few other waters in Virginia host all three of the bass. Also present are several members of the sunfish family, including the popular bluegill. Channel catfish, crappie, muskellunge, rock bass, and walleyes also fin its clear, cool waters. The catfish, muskellunge, and walleyes are stocked annually, but all of the other fish populations are self-sustaining. Maps showing the established locations of the walleye populations are posted on the bulletin board near the boat ramp. Fish structures of various kinds have been established at various points throughout the lake. A large rock reef has been established near the picnic area and is easily accessible to bank anglers. Fishing facilities are excellent, including rental boats, a boat-launching ramp, and a fishing platform located near the upper end of the lake. The lake is open 24 hours a day though the park closes at 10 P.M. For additional information, call the park office at (276) 783-3422 or contact the Marion office of the Virginia Department of Game and Inland Fisheries, 1796 Highway Sixteen, Marion, VA 24354, telephone (276) 783-4860, or the Division of Parks and Recreation at the address given below.

SWIFT CREEK LAKE

Swift Creek Lake is a 107-acre impoundment in the Pocahontas State Park in Chesterfield County. There is also a smaller

10-acre body of water known as Beaver Lake that has no rental boats or boat-launching ramp but is open to bank fishing. Swift Creek Lake, however, has rental boats and a launching ramp for private boats. The fishing hours are posted on the lake. They may vary from summer to winter. The lake has a good population of introduced largemouth bass, bluegills, catfish, and red-ear sunfish. The native chain pickerel are plentiful in this small lake and offer some exciting fishing. The lake is shallow near the boat ramp but gradually deepens toward the dam. For additional information, contact the park at (804) 796-4255 or the Division of Parks and Recreation at the address give below.

TWIN LAKES STATE PARK LAKES

A pair of lakes, Goodwin and Prince Edward, are the major attractions in the Twin Lakes State Park in Prince Edward County. Among the recreational opportunities they offer is good fishing for largemouth bass, channel catfish, crappie, and bluegills and other sunfish. Lake Goodwin is a 14-acre lake, and Prince Edward is larger at 35 acres. Grass carp have been introduced in an effort to control the aquatic vegetation, and fish structures have been placed at appropriate places in the lake. Both lakes have boat-launching ramps and rental boats. For additional information, contact the park at (434) 392-3435, or the Division of Parks and Recreation at the address given below.

OTHER STATE PARK WATERS

There are small ponds or lakes in several other state parks. In Sky Meadows State Park in Fauquier County, there is a small pond of approximately an acre that offers good fishing. There are no facilities such as boat ramps or fishing piers, but a light boat or canoe can be launched from the shore. The pond has good populations of largemouth bass and bluegills. In the York

River State Park, there is a small 7-acre impoundment that offers fishing for largemouth bass and bluegills. Rental boats are available, or an angler can fish from fishing piers. Information on both of these angling possibilities can be obtained by contacting the Division of Parks and Recreation at the address given below.

> Virginia Division of Parks and Recreation
> 4010 West Broad Street
> Richmond, VA 23230-1104
> Telephone (804) 367-1000

There are numerous other still waters in Virginia and scattered across the state. Included are farm ponds, most of which are privately owned but often open to fishing upon a courteous request; city and county reservoirs; and a number of small ponds or lakes in the George Washington and Jefferson National Forests. Many of the latter are trout waters stocked periodically. The best way to locate these waters is to contact the Virginia Department of Game and Inland Fisheries, 4010 West Broad Street, Richmond, VA 23230-1104; or telephone (804) 367-1000 and ask for the Fisheries Division, or better still ask for the regional office in the area you are interested in fishing. Sometimes, simply driving through the backcountry, locating bodies of still water, and then running down the owner, be it a farmer, city, or county, and seeking permission to fish is the best way. Often a permit is required, for which there might be a modest fee.

The Virginia angler who asserts a little effort can probably locate some of the best lake fishing in America.

Index